All That
We Are
We
Give

All That We Are We Give

James G. T. Fairfield

HERALD PRESS
Scottdale, Pennsylvania
Kitchener, Ontario

Library of Congress Cataloging in Publication Data

Fairfield, James G T 1926-
All that we are we give.

Bibliography: p.
1. Christian life—1960-   2. Stewardship, Christian. I. Title.
BV4501.2.F28   248'.4   77-14510
ISBN 0-8361-1839-1

ALL THAT WE ARE WE GIVE
Copyright© 1977 by Herald Press, Scottdale, Pa. 15683
    Published simultaneously in Canada by Herald Press,
    Kitchener, Ont. N2G 4M5
Library of Congress Catalog Card Number: 77-14510
International Standard Book Number: 0-8361-1839-1
Printed in the United States of America
Design: Alice B. Shetler

10 9 8 7 6 5 4 8

From James and Norma,

to the caring people of
Lindale Mennonite Church,
with our gratitude

A lifestyle for mission—

> If you know who and what
> you are, you have the
> potential—within the
> fellowship of faith—to
> change your world for the
> better.

Contents

Preliminary overview

How can we live more effectively both as persons and as members of the fellowship of faith? This has never been easy and in a world as complex and as troubled as ours today, the prospects for a simplified (focused) lifestyle are even more obscure.

In the technological world we had previously come to accept, we now have scientists and environmentalists telling us we have gone too far. Yet how can we readjust our energy-intensified lives to assure ourselves that we are not at war with God and His creation?

Furthermore, as our technology multiplies, the rich seem to get richer, and the poor nations poorer. For the people of God, our affluent consumption in the face of impoverished need seems to turn the words of Jesus against us.

Yet what can any one of us do? We can barely cope with the day-to-day struggles of our own lives. How can God expect us to give of ourselves for so many others? Particularly when the needs are so great?

All That We Are We Give opens up new ways for us to change ourselves and the world we live in. Instead of being squeezed into a mold of social conformity, we *can* break out together and become—as we were meant to be—people with an effective and fulfilling lifestyle.

Today as in the past the potential for positive redirection in the world lies with the church, the people of God. This kingdom within the world's kingdoms has a mandate from its Master: to be the agents of reconciling action between His purposes for all creation and those of us who haven't yet got the hang of what His reality is all about.

To be positive change-agents we must uncover our talents and release our resources. Together in the church (specifically in our local congregations) we have the job of becoming all we should be by the grace of God. And not just for ourselves. But also in order that as the community of faith we might be more effective ministers of His renewing grace to the world.

To help us understand ourselves and our relationship to the world's needs, Part I brings new insights into the backgrounds of our human dilemma, spiritually, ecologically, and economically.

In Part II a number of practical methods of discovering latent talents and abilities are outlined. With suggested materials for group use, local congregations can develop programs to help members combine their gifts, interests, and opportunities into a lifestyle for mission to the world.

Then in Part III this through-the-week lifestyle is broken down into its material elements. Christlike integrity will change our approach to earning power, how we spend what we earn, what we save for our own future—all as part of the total giving of ourselves and our resources within the reinforcing strength of the community of God.

The purposes of this book are threefold. As a study book it is designed to help you find yourself and your place as a change-agent within the kingdom of God. It can also be used in a group process to strengthen the ability of the local church to assist its members in their search for a fulfilling lifestyle.

And it is meant to help the reader review the essential value today of the community of faith as the living presence of God in His world.

The material is arranged to serve both leisurely individual reading as well as group study. Questions in the text can stimulate individual study as well as group discussion. The transition between chapters is meant to reinforce your personal discoveries in the preceding material. It will also serve as a guide for leading a group study in the chapter to follow.

For a discussion leader:

1. You will need to read through the book well ahead of time so you can absorb where it is going.

2. Then use the "To" section of the transition page ahead of each chapter as a basis for developing your plans for studying the chapter.

3. The questions throughout the chapter and those in the "From" section of the transition page at the end can help you involve the group in discussion and discovery.

4. Participants in discussion groups or Sunday school classes using this book should be encouraged to read each chapter before the session. Key portions or ideas could profitably be read in the sessions.

The Board of Congregational Ministries of the Mennonite Church commissioned the book. Initial planning came from the Commission on Congregational Planning and Resources: Glen Horst, Dorothy Yoder Nyce, Macler Shepard, Ivan J. Kauffmann, Dwight Stoltzfus, and Jason Martin. Their concerns were sharpened further by

a task force including Joyce Hostetler, Evelyn Shellen-
berger, Willard Roth, Laurence Martin, David Helmuth,
Howard Zehr, and Harold Bauman.

Transition
From—Preliminary overview

What percentage of your life is spent in satisfying
activity? If you are like most of us you do not ask yourself
such a question in case the answer is too frustrating. Because most of us have not had a choice—we do what we do
because of factors other than personal preference. But what
if that could change? What direction would you choose for
your life? And for what reasons?

To—Part 1, Chapter 1, Where have we been?

History holds meaning for the world in which we find
ourselves today. Assuming a purpose in creation, we can
also assume a purpose for humanity and for our lives now as
the "royalty of creation." Yet we have failed ourselves and
creation in so many ways—why?

In Chapter 1 we will establish a brief framework for the
historical development of our present situation. And our
uneasiness at world problems. See Genesis 1, 2, and 3.

Part 1, Chapter 1—Where have we been?
A. The purposes of God in creation.
    1. Beliefs about creation.
    2. Humanity: lords of creation (Genesis 1 and 2).
        a. First-man's rebellion (Genesis 3).
        b. Our rebellion today.
    3. God's purpose in creation today:
    to return us to a responsible
    lifestyle in the church of Christ.
B. Christian concerns with man's rebellion illustrated.
    1. Concern for future of the world.
    2. Concern for personal ineffectiveness.
    3. Concern for the church's ineffectiveness.

Part I

The Background of Power:
Which Lifestyle for Mission?

1
Where have we been?

I do dimly perceive that whilst everything around us is ever changing, ever dying, there is underlying all that change, a living power that is changeless, that holds all together. . . . I can see that in the midst of death life persists, in the midst of untruth truth persists, in the midst of darkness light persists. Hence I gather that God is Life, Truth, Light. He is Love, He is the Supreme Good. But he is no God who merely satisfies the intellect if he ever does. God to be God must rule the heart and transform it.

—*M.K. Gandhi*

Is there purpose in creation? Or purposelessness? Whichever answer you have chosen in the past has become a part of your life today.

Let's assume that God's activity in creation means more than a beginning to the world. But is it ultimately for us a defeat or a victory? Will creation fail at our hand as some insist it is doing now? Or is creation purposeful and accomplishing a goal?

In general, humanity holds two beliefs about creation. first, that creation happened and is playing out a game of chance. Evolution has exhausted itself in man and man is exhausting creation through careless overpopulation and overpollution. We are not only overfilling our nest but we are soiling it and tearing it apart in wanton vandalism that must soon end.

Alternatively, creation is seen as going somewhere, and in the providence of God has somewhere to go. God has not only initiated creation, but continues to supervise its development as the incubus of a new creation.

What direction might this take in the future? One idea is that enough humanity may achieve enough maturity in Christ soon enough to restore some balance to nature and some capability of living in harmony with the earth. This calls for a stabilized use of resources by a population with zero growth.

Or second, as the earth is wasted, humanity may push out to live on satellite colonies in orbit around the earth. Or on a new heaven and earth, wherever and whatever that may mean in space travel to new galaxies.

Or finally, Christ's return may bring judgment through our vandalism. A terrible cleansing by fire may lead to a new act of creation involving the earth and the universe we now inhabit.

> For further study if you choose: Which one of these future possibilities allows for the historical conditions of the world as you understand them? What biblical evidence can you find which lends support to each? See Matthew 24; Romans 8:18-25; 2 Peter 3; Revelation 21.

Whatever the future of the earth and her resources, the interdependence of creation has always focused in humanity as the lords of creation. In Genesis 1 and 2 that doctrine is laid out as a charge given by God for His purpose. The naming of names (Genesis 2:19, 20) became the first act of dominion—seemingly to give place and position and function to all living beings. (We do a similar thing today. The prominent Jeep is now named from its military intention: GP—General Purpose vehicle. Like the people's car—Volkswagen).

But the first chapters of Genesis record more than humanity's responsibility to identify and manage the created world. It records the beginnings of man's mismanagement also, the use of resources for something other than which they were intended. There are trees whose fruits are beneficial to the body—but there are others whose eating means sickness and death. "First-man" ignored the directions of God and ate his own choice of diet. He won himself spiritual separation from God. We have inherited not only his willful choice to distance himself from God but also his spiritual death as well.

Whatever else first-man's rebellion revealed, it proved the significance of the greatest gift of God: the freedom of our wills. We are free to choose faith or unfaith, righteousness or unrighteousness.

The history of our freedom also reveals our choices: some good, many evil. There is no guarantee in freedom that we will choose the good. On the contrary, the momentum of choices down the ages seems to guarantee that we will choose selfishly rather than rightly.

So it seems we choose first to suit ourselves. We develop our lifestyle around our choices. And a great many people today build their lifestyles with little or no consideration of the direction or choices God would have us select.

We eat a diet that modern advertising encourages. We begin to smoke, not because it is good for us, but because it is a socially approved initiation rite. We continue to strip-mine coal because it is necessary in the short run, even though the scars on the land are permanently devastating. And we choose to risk our environment with Kepone and other untested chemicals because it is more profitable to sell without testing—until disaster strikes.

It may be that the pessimists are right, and the earth will die at our hands. If so, it will be an agonizing death for nature—and for us.

But is the purpose of the world to run down and collapse through our mismanagement? Or is it to cooperate with God's love in bringing us to our senses and to help us rediscover our responsibility together as the royalty of creation? Then to return us to a close, interested participation in a lifestyle that befits the kin (*kinder* or children) of God?

So God's redeeming work in Jesus Christ takes on new significance for today's living patterns. Christ not only saves us from the destructive power of our sins but He also wins us back to the creatively balanced lifestyle which is God's—a lifestyle of belonging in the creative family of faith which is the church of Christ.

The Apostle Paul called it the mystery of the ages, hidden in the confused history of man's betrayal of his responsibility. Appropriated by faith, it is "Christ in you, the hope of glory." God's answer to our confusion is the remarkable experience of being remade by the Spirit of God into usefulness and fulfillment once again.

God has not left us to blunder on alone in our bewildering world. There is a reality which moves along with us in our unreality, reaching across to us constantly with the freeing word of hope: "Trust God. Lean not on

your own insufficient understanding, but commit your
way to Him and He will make things clear" (Proverbs
3:5, 6, paraphrased).

   To speak of "simplifying our lifestyle" is to risk
misunderstanding. For many people the phrase has come
to mean natural foods and a countercultural movement
back to rural living.

   But a simplified lifestyle today includes many options
for the city apartment dweller as well as the rural land-
owner. It is more an attitude and a commitment than a
place and a diet. It is a *focused* lifestyle.

   The King James Version of the Bible uses the term
"love of the world" to describe a life that is *not* simple.
But who chooses deliberately to complicate his life? And
where does simple end and complex begin?

   Eric is a rising young lawyer. He has a clientele of
small businesses and a growing number of corporations.
When he joined his law firm as a junior, his wife
recognized his need to put in long hours in order to get
himself established in the community.°

   Now that his practice is established Eric continues to
work long hours, partly because he likes his work and
partly because his early uncertainties wore a groove in his
personality. He has a drive to work, or the drive to work
has him.

   Eric and Paula have two children, a four-acre "estate,"
and the comforts which fall to a $30,000 salary plus

°While the personal experiences mentioned in this book are based
on actual testimony, most of the names and situations used are fic-
titious and often include the combined experiences of several individuals.

benefits. But the price of their lifestyle is beginning to disturb them.

"We love our home and neighborhood," Paula insists, "so it isn't a matter of wanting to change. Yet for all that we do have, we are both conscious of something missing. But what that might mean in changing what we are doing or how we should live—we haven't been able to figure out."

Eric doesn't have as clear a sense of lack as Paula. But he has read *Future Shock* and seen Jacques Cousteau on television warn that the ocean will soon be dead—and his conscience nags him about his share in creating the world's problems.

His work gives him some sense of mission—as does Paula's involvement in local politics. And both are active in a suburban church. Paula is primary superintendent in their congregation's educational program. Eric continues as a consultant to an inner-city mission he worked with as a college student.

"Jesus Christ is important to my life," Eric confides. "I feel that His guidance is very necessary to my professional career as well as in family life."

Why then the uneasy feeling of something wrong with their lives? For Paula and Eric the North American dream has come true. Health, happiness, and prosperity pursue them relentlessly. Even God is on their side. Are they simply overstimulated dilettantes? Are they reacting like overindulged children who, having everything, want more?

But neither of these indictments describes either their attitudes or their feelings accurately. If pushed to analyze the inner uneasiness which disturbs their happiness, Paula confesses to feelings of guilt. "We have and use more than we need, and that's wrong," she insists.

On the other hand Eric vehemently denies the guilt she wants him to share, and reacts with some anger at Paula's feelings about their possessions.

"Nobody's going to lay a guilt trip on me for achieving some success in my profession. I've worked hard and earned everything we have."

But in Bible class discussions, Eric has ceased his automatic defenses of free enterprise and laissez-faire economics which he used to offer freely in the past. While these still appeal to him, he admits to their failure too, "just as welfare economics has failed," he explains. But he is disturbed at the inability of rational modern governments to deal adequately with the problems of the world.

And he is deeply disturbed—along with Paula—that nothing is being done about it. "Not even by the church," he points out. And the failure of the church— their church and their congregation—disturbs them most of all.

Eric and Paula are fortunate in their uneasiness. At least they are aware of a discord of spirit and will not be satisfied until some changes are made.

And perhaps the church—including their own congregation—has not failed them and the world as much as they fear.

The church has long been blamed for not doing enough about the world and its condition. These stones of judgment have been cast from all sides. "You Christians are all alike. You preach change but won't give us the tools to do the job." Or: "Tools, tools! All you give us are tools. Why don't you give us yourselves?" Or, "You give us yourselves? But we don't want to be like you—we

want to solve our own problems our own way! Go
home!"

'Twas ever thus. And ever will be so. Jesus experienced
the infuriating frustration of healing the blind—then being dared to perform a miracle in order to prove Himself.
But Jesus successfully ignored the dares and went on
with His work, "to do the will of him who sent me."

So does the church. And in spite of its struggles the
church has managed to go on with its business in ways
which have proved effective in the world of its time.

And that is what is happening today.

Transition
From—Where have we been?

What are the purposes God might have for your life?
What do you perceive might be the blocks in achieving
those purposes? Who or what is holding you back? Where
might God begin to change your circumstances? To change
you? What new directions might He wish for your life?

Consider some evidences from recent history which point
to humanity's moral or social improvement; others which
suggest social and spiritual failure.

What has "church" meant to you in the past? How might
it help you in the future?

To—Chapter 2, Where are our environments taking us?

Our environments today exert a tremendous influence on
the lifestyle we choose. There are at least two environments:
the primary or natural world, and the secondary structures
we have built around us. Too often we find ourselves willing
captives of the world we have created and at war with God's
creation. And in so doing we frustrate the goal God has for
us, which is to be renewed in Christ and to mature in His
likeness.

In Chapter 2 we will consider and accept God's goal for
us—for the purposes of this book if not yet for our lives. And

as part of this commitment, we will increase our convictions to work for a better natural environment. See Acts 19; Ephesians 1; 1 John 1:2-4.

Chapter 2—Where are our environments taking us?

A. Today's environmental problems reviewed.
  1. The dissolution of social purpose.
  2. The dehumanizing of technology.
  3. Primary and secondary environments.
      a. Primary environment problems illustrated.
      b. Shift to secondary environments illustrated.
  4. Failure of technology with environments.

B. How our lifestyle influences environments.
  1. North Americans model irresponsibility.
  2. Christians (becomers-like-God) exhibit responsible action.
      a. The environment of Ephesus in New Testament times.
      b. Paul explains God's purpose for Christians in Ephesus (Ephesians 1).
  3. Christians are revealers and defenders of life (1 John 1).

2
Where are our environments taking us?

One of the very few things in life that I have learned is that no question is more futile than: "Can one man do anything?" One man can do everything. And no man can take the responsibility for undervaluing what he may do.

One thing he can do is to connect his convictions to those of others. You get a multiplying power as you connect those ideas to the ideas of others. . . .

A lot depends on what we think is important. The question therefore is not what one man can do but whether one man thinks that what he believes in is important enough to tie himself to it and to let his actions reflect those beliefs.

—*Norman Cousins*

Before we can more fully understand God's purpose for us individually, we must more fully grasp what He intends for His people together. And why He has a job for us to do in our environments today.

Many thoughtful people reject the idea of purpose in creation. The swings of history and the failures of so many good intentions for humanity seem to point to despair rather than to hope. "We are a defeated people," this seems to say. "We are headed nowhere but oblivion. There is no future but chaos."

Despair and alienation are too much the product of our time. It seems incredible that so many preteen children should be driven to suicide each year in our world—but cold as the statistics of suicide may be, the reality of widespread despair is much more disturbing.

Why have we abandoned purpose? History may some-day suggest an answer for the twentieth century. Certainly our period will be looked upon as a time of precipitous change, when technology developed so quickly it left much of humanity behind.

We seem to have moved too swiftly for our spirits. As beings capable of making decisions, we have made the mechanical choices rather than the moral ones. We can build an automobile on an assembly line in a few hours. But in the hours and days that a line worker becomes part of his machine, he also becomes that much less of a human.

> Take a survey: What is the most likely source of depression to you in your lifestyle? How might it be changed?

The swift advance of technology has left our processes of education and moral training in limbo. We have become clever innovators. In a few years we have become so medically sophisticated we can keep a dead person alive. And we can abort life so simply that it is done hundreds of times every day. But we have also abandoned to our technology the too-difficult decisions of who shall live while dying, and who must die while trying to come alive.

Consider also where we have come to in relation to our physical or *primary environment*. In times past, human-kind lived more intimately and harmoniously with the land, the sea, and the air. And change moved in the deliberate frame of the seasons.

Today we find ourselves enmeshed in ever-shifting

secondary environments: shopping plazas, cars and high-ways, factory work areas, offices, all-electric homes. And we must live up to these or lose our uncertain place in the book of today's life.

> Can you identify the secondary environments which mean the most to you? Which are least helpful? Are they beyond your control? What might God want you to learn from them about the world? About yourself?

Harold Williamson lives in a walk-up in the Bronx. He and Joanne both work at a trucking terminal and are taking night classes together at City College of New York.

They were married just before Manhattan's garbage strike and it was a smelly introduction to wedded bliss, sleeping only three floors up from a mounting heap of cabbage and disposable diapers and chicken bones.

Strangely enough, that's when they became environmentalists. As the garbage grew higher and more noisome, Joanne and Harold spent more time at the CCNY library. And so did their friends.

Garbage talk shifted around to what to do with the stuff. And gradually Joanne became aware of the much larger problem than that of the stinking pile under her window.

"We are dumping our garbage in the ocean, just out there," she points vaguely eastward. Her voice trembles with indignation in her new awareness. "That gets it off our streets all right, but now we're killing the ocean with all our muck."

"The thing is," Harold adds, "we're more concerned with our streets than with the primary environment. We never think about that big raft of garbage floating out there. It's in somebody else's ocean, not ours."

"You grow up thinking your street, your neighborhood, is all there is to the world," Joanne joins in. "Like our neighbor's kid. He won't drink milk now that his teacher has told him it comes from a cow instead of a store. Because the store was part of his known world, familiar and safe."

In several ways we have abandoned our primary environment to serve our secondary institutions—and not just in North America. Like Alabama blacks and Saskatchewan young people, the rural residents of the world have been moving to the city and its secondary environments.

"This shift from the land to the city is worldwide and is accelerating and its environmental consequences— overcrowding, pollution, unemployment, deteriorating public services, and depletion of resources—are acutely important in the lives of all peoples, whether they live in dwindling rural settlements or in sprawling urban centres" (from the report on Habitat, the United Nations Conference/Exposition on Human Settlements held recently in Vancouver, and detailed in Issue No. 4, 1976, of the Commercial Letter, Canadian Imperial Bank of Commerce).

Nine major issues dominated Habitat discussions:
1. Man-made and natural environments.
2. Social justice and the question of differing values and cultures.
3. Land use and ownership.
4. Rural development.
5. National settlement policies.
6. Sharing and managing world resources.

7. Appropriate technology.
8. People's participation in planning and implementation.
9. Community action for a better habitat.

The first major document to come out of the Habitat Conference called on national governments to work at improving their own environments. The focus: land reform and reversing urban sprawl, with emphasis on providing land, water, and housing for the poor. A second focus raised the specter of swiftly diminishing natural resources.

> In your community, which of the world problems listed by Habitat seems the most demanding? What in your lifestyle may help improve the situation?

You would think we'd know better here in North America. We have the technological know-how to make changes for the better. And we've had the environmentalists to warn us where we've been going. But, like the U.S. surgeon-general's cautions on a pack of cigarettes, the environmentalists' warnings have been only partially effective.

Why else would we build so many buildings and parking lots and highways in the Niagara Peninsula? This strip of land between Hamilton and Buffalo is Canada's "fruit belt," one of the most fertile agricultural areas in the world, but has almost become an industrial area instead.

Our primary environment, instead of a partner in our mutual subsistence, is still looked upon as a potential for profit and capital gains.

As children in Manitoba school festivals we sang, "O Shenandoah," and longed to see this famous river. Now my wife and I live in the Shenandoah Valley, famed "breadbasket of the Confederacy," and know how quickly it is losing its agricultural potential to indiscriminate development. "Land use" reform is now being pushed by legislative action. But many valley farmers and landowners are fighting reform. Instead they vigorously defend their freedom to profit from pavement, as others before them have done.

Where are we now? We are still developing in North America a lifestyle that is not the best example, either for ourselves or the rest of the world, of how to live with our environments.

Then where are we going? With our basic assumption that God cares for His world, where is He taking us?

The purpose of God's history is recovery or redemption, not the chaos and despair we see around us. In spite of the times, there is now as always a continuity of grace. God is working out His purpose in His creation and His people.

Mind you, humankind has paid little attention to the self-revealing works of God. We've been too busy trying to tell God what we think should be done instead.

Ever since the beginning, we have pleaded with our own images of God in order to satisfy our desires. We plead for rain on our crops. For less rain. To gain better health. Or, as Linus explains to Charlie Brown, "to be rich and famous and handsome—and humble."

But God has a greater objective for us. From the beginning, or as the Bible puts it, "from the foundation of the world," we were meant to be "becomers-like-God."

As Genesis 1 records the seven-day celebration of creation, it focuses on the final act of God: "Let us make man in our image, after our likeness." In the fellowship of God and His people each one of us has the potential, by faith, to mature into the likeness of God. And by the grace of God our environments can cooperate with faith in helping that process.

That we do not always grow into the image of God which He showed us so intimately in Jesus is certainly not His fault. The world has grown full of people with little interest in "becoming like God." We would prefer God to become like us, to get on our team and stop being a drag on our progress.

But God has not abandoned His purpose or His creation. God's character, so clearly revealed in Jesus, still calls us from our dark progress into His renewing light; from our lonely individualism into His loving community. This is for all creation's benefit as well as our own.

> What characteristics of God which Jesus revealed might be the most helpful ones to deal with the environmental problems in your community? Are the characteristics available in your group? If not, why not?

The Apostle Paul, writing to the Christians at Ephesus, gave them a clear picture of their calling. At the time, Ephesus was a glittering example of the world's advances: commercial capital of Asia, on the main highway from Rome to the East, with marbled streets, a magnificent 50,000-seat amphitheater for Greek plays and games, a marketplace to rival our biggest shopping plazas—and the temple of Artemis, one of the seven wonders of the ancient world, to reinforce the status quo.

Artemis, goddess of nature, nearly cost Paul his life. The new Christians Paul was teaching had stopped buying the souvenirs and Artemis charms, and this threatened the income of the cultic trade. (See Acts 19.) The ensuing riot nearly finished Paul's career.

When Paul later wrote the Ephesian Christians, it was to remind them of the great purpose of God being worked out in them, in spite of the tensions their new lifestyle might create with their neighbors: "For he has made known to us in all wisdom and insight the mystery of his will, according to his purpose which he set forth in Christ as a plan for the fulness of time, to unite all things in him, things in heaven and things on earth" (Ephesians 1:9, 10, RSV).

In becoming like God we become part of a great uniting redeeming work, which is His will and objective for our lives and for His world.

The span of our life is a kindergarten for the kingdom of God. We believe what God has shown us in Jesus Christ and through His body the church. And as we begin to act on that belief by faith we begin the slow transformation back from the character the world has stamped upon us, and into the character of godlikeness. We are born again and the new person that begins its growth is a child of God, called to His unifying redeeming work in the company of His people.

Our maturation begins here on earth in the environment God has provided and graduates from this kindergarten into the mature resurrected life of heaven. We know little of the environment of heaven, but we can know much of its character as we join with its people in God's kingdom now coming alive in the world.

"For it was *life* which appeared before us: we saw it, we are eyewitnesses of it, and are now writing to you about it. It was the very life of all ages, the life that has always existed with God the Father, which actually became visible in person to us mortal men. We repeat, we really saw and heard what we are now writing to you about. We want you to be with us in this—in this fellowship with God the Father, and Jesus Christ his Son. We must write and tell you about it, because the more that fellowship extends, the greater the joy it brings to us who are already in it" (1 John 1:2-4, Phillips).

This then is our call: to choose God's way instead of the world's. To commit ourselves to His lifestyle as revealed in Christ Jesus. To join in the maturing work of His people in the church, the visible kingdom of God. To defend creation and God's purpose through it. And to share in His loving acts toward the world He is seeking to redeem.

Transition
From—Where are our environments taking us?

Which products used in your home come from your local primary environment? Which from another part of the world? How much of these primary products have secondary packaging and preparation?

What immediate steps would be necessary for you to take if your secondary environment should fail (power went off, transportation stopped, etc.)? How might you work together as a congregation. For immediate survival—and for long-term goals? What other groups of people share your concern? Formulate six or more positive actions which need to be taken in your community. Add a similar list of actions for the nation, then for the world as a whole. Then list the people you know right now whom you could call to act upon your suggestions. Consult your local officials for names of others to whom to send your recommendations.

To—Chapter 3, Where is our affluent lifestyle leading us?

As much as we have failed to exercise good stewardship of our primary environment, we have also failed each other. The citizens of the world are virtually our brothers and sisters, yet we have developed lifestyles in competition with them rather than cooperation in mutual esteem and interest.

Has North American development raced beyond the point of no return for the rest of the world? Statistics may now point to the fatal overuse of available resources by "developed" countries at the expense of the poorer nations.

Furthermore, the people of God have participated in the widening gap between rich and poor.

In Chapter 3 you can compare your thinking to the suggestion that a change in our lifestyle must become a priority so that we can (1) model a zero drain on the peoples and resources of the world and (2) help each other make a positive contribution to the world of the resources that we ourselves are meant to be as the people of God. See Isaiah 3:14, 15; Amos 5:11, 21-24; Matthew 6:25-33; Mark 10:17-25; Ephesians 4:2-6, 11-13.

Chapter 3—Where is our affluent lifestyle leading us?

A. The widening gap between rich nations and poor.
     1. Advantage lies in power over wages.
     2. Failure of "development" for poor nations.
     3. Failure of aid programs.

B. The problem of wealth for the people of God.
     1. Christian ambivalence to problems illustrated.
     2. Jesus teaches wealth cannot replace faith (Mark 10:17-25; Matthew 6:25-33).
     3. Old Testament teachings on oppression of the poor (Isaiah 3:14, 15; Amos 5:11, 21-24).

C. The Christian acts in contrast to affluent advantage.
     1. Uncover talents with aid of church.
     2. Develop a simplified lifestyle.
     3. Put talents and lifestyle at disposal of Christ and His kingdom (Ephesians 4:2-6, 11-13).

3
Where is our affluent lifestyle leading us?

Great fortunes were built on the exploitation of Appalachian workers and Appalachian resources, yet the land was left without revenues to care for its social needs, like education, welfare, old age, and illness.

Some may say "that's economics" but we say that economics is made by people. Its principles don't fall down from the sky and remain for all eternity. Those who claim they are prisoners of the law of economics only testify that they are prisoners of the idol. The same thing which is so obvious in Appalachia goes on outside the mountains. Plain people work hard all their life, and their parents before them, yet they can't make ends meet.

Food is too expensive.

Taxes are too high for most.

(Too low for the rich.)

Sickness puts people into debt.

College is out of reach for their children.

Paychecks keep shrinking.

And it's still worse for those who can't work, especially the elderly. . . .

It is the mountain's spirit of resistance which must be defended at any cost, for at stake is the spirit of all humanity. There are too few spaces of soul left in our lives. . . . Now an alien culture battles to shape us into plastic forms empty of spirit, into beasts of burden, without mystery.

—From "This Land Is Home to Me," a pastoral letter by the 24 Catholic bishops of Appalachia, in *The Mountain Eagle*.

In the context of a polluted primary environment and the distortions of our secondary environments, we have seen that God has a purpose for us. And not as individuals only but as fully participating members of His working body, the church.

But where will this take us in relation to the other peoples of the world? Particularly since we are among the secure and well-fed minority?

For instance, why have we been born in North America and not Bangladesh? Many of us might answer, "To enjoy the good life, and praise it forever." But few of us would appreciate being accused of doing so at the expense of someone else.

Yet it can be shown that our North American lifestyle depends heavily upon the long hours of labor and low wages of workers in the poorer nations of the world.

In order to maintain a growth economy, we need enormous quantities of raw materials, most from the poorer nations. And we must buy them at a price advantage. Consequently, if the standard of living were to rise in the countries where we buy aluminum ore or coffee or tin or sugar, then our economy and our lifestyle would be threatened.

Our economic structure has grown to depend on keeping a difference between our wages and theirs. Since we have never lost that competitive edge, we don't know what would happen if we did. But we fear that our lifestyle must move downward to meet theirs on the way up. And over the years our government has institutionalized our fears by shaping national and foreign economic policies to our continuing advantage—with the willing assent of the governed.

Yet our policies have generated an embarrassment of

wealth. In our extravagance we throw away more food than many Fourth World nations eat. We use ⅓ of the oil, ⅓ of the gas, almost half the coal, and most of the atomic energy in the world. We import enormous quantities of diminishing resources. And in the past we have propped up dictatorial governments who will feed our voracious appetite for these resources.

Then to justify our appetite we talk of "development" for the poorer countries as a way to raise their standard of living without threat to our own. It is an exciting idea for the poor peoples of the world and until recently has kept them and us from seeing its impossibility.

Statistically the dream is incredible. The U.S. comprises only 6 percent of the world's population. If only 14 percent of the rest of the world were to join us in our current rate of consumption, there would be—both literally and absolutely—nothing left of the world's known resources for the other 80 percent to use in their development.°

If these statistics are only half right, the implications for our future are not reassuring. Furthermore, if the people of God are to help change the situation, we'll need to be sure from whom we're taking our directions— whether the leading of God, or the leading economic indicators.

Take a survey: Do you or do you not believe the statistics of shortages? How much of a credibility gap exists between pessimistic forecasts and our comfortable optimism? If the

---

°Statistics in this chapter from the Clergy and Laity Concerned, Project on Hunger, published in *Another Newsletter*, New York, December 1976, and "What Next in Africa?" articles in *Atlas Magazine*, June 1976.

statistics are true, what more is needed to convince us of the world's peril?

A second bottom-line figure we must deal with is that instead of things improving for the poor of the world in recent years, their condition is actually worsening. This is true even of Brazil, one of the Third World countries which is looked upon as a model of development. After five years with one of the highest economic growth rates in the world, Brazil's economic minister estimated recently that only 5 percent had "developed" a better lifestyle. The rest of the population had barely managed to hold their own. And the standard of living of 45 percent had actually worsened.

But what about North American generosity? Are not our aid programs enough to lift the lives of the poor?

Three decades ago in the years of the Marshall Plan we believed in that dream. But not today. Too many of us are now disillusioned by the corruption in programs which have been administered through government channels. We seem only to have created a new class of "relief barons" who have turned relief materials and funds to their own profit. Even some Christian relief programs in recent years have been tarred with an uneven political brush, which has been hard for us to accept.

Futhermore, some of our aid programs have backfired. Leonard Siemens is associate dean of agriculture at the University of Manitoba and a director of Mennonite Central Committee. In a *Gospel Herald* interview Siemens tells what he saw happening with relief wheat sent to poor countries. "The domestic price sinks to such a low level that the local farmers have very little incentive to produce.

"Their own fields often go barren . . . or worse still,

(are) seeded with 'cash crops' for the North American market like coffee, sugar, or rubber—because they cannot afford to produce food for themselves at the low price at which it arrives from overseas."

So there is more to the poverty problem than shiploads of surplus grain and relief commodities. The situation is much more complex and frustrating. Yet the lives of the poor cry out to the love of God in our hearts, awaiting the decisions and actions of our minds and hands.

"It hurts to be looked on as a 'fat cat' simply because we live in North America," Ortney Hess protests. "I work hard enough for what I make and I look around and see ablebodied people on welfare.

"Look at the JOBS column in the paper! There are all kinds of jobs going begging. That really makes me mad!

"And I've got a gut feeling it's the same over in Africa or India. If people worked at whatever they can find to do, like the Bible says, we wouldn't have all this fighting and complaining about oppression."

Ortney isn't alone in his feelings. He's a good Christian businessman, a tithing member of the Mennonite Church on the edge of town. And other men in his congregation would say "Amen" to his reaction. There are no Cadillacs in the church parking lot, because such ostentation would not fit with their idea of Christian stewardship. But their cars are comfortably well equipped, with several high-priced models in evidence.

So what is their responsibility? The members of this congregation ardently oppose the oppression of the poor. Most give generously to relief and to missions. How then can they be held in any way accountable for the poverty in Bangladesh or the lack of development in Haiti?

· Of course they are not *directly* responsible, any more than any other well-intentioned North American citizen. And this makes it difficult to feel any personal need to take action. If we are not responsible personally for the economic policies which make our life so pleasant, why not relax and enjoy it?

Furthermore, consumer economists argue that if we didn't consume what the poor nations ship to us, they would be deeper in poverty than ever. So it would seem our duty from this point of view to use up even more of their fast-dimishing resources.

Except for the economic advantage we command. Hence our greater consumption has meant more profit for us, less benefit for them. So instead of narrowing, the gap continues to grow even wider between the rich and the poor. And somehow, in some way, we who do not wish to be responsible find ourselves inextricably involved.

Jesus said, "The poor you always have with you." Why? Is it because (a) the poor are a lesser breed? Or (b) they are accursed of God? Or (c) advantage has been denied to them? Or (d) the world system of selfishness demands that someone be at the bottom of the ladder? What reasons occur to you?

It is possible for us to spiritualize the problems and needs of the poor. We cancel their demands on our lives by burying our sensitivities in a job or avocation or simply in the good life. Even religion can become more to us than caring. And our eyes and ears grow dull to the anguish of reality. Even if we meet it face-to-face, as did the wealthy young religious leader who stopped Jesus on the road one day (Mark 10:17-25).

"Teacher," he asked, "what good act can I do to ensure that I will have eternal life?" Jesus gave him an answer in the man's own self-conscious terms: "You know the commandments. Do not commit adultery, do not murder, do not steal, do not bear false witness, honor your father and mother."

But the man was aware of a lack in his reality that keeping commandments had not satisfied. "I have kept all these carefully from the time I was a youth," he replied.

Then Jesus surprised him with totally unexpected advice, "One thing you have missed. Sell everything you own and give the money to the poor, and you will be rich in heaven.

"Then come and follow me."

At these words, the man's eyes fell, because he was very rich. When Jesus saw his look, He said, "How hard it is for those who are wealthy to enter the kingdom of God. It is easier for a camel to go through the eye of a needle!"

The young leader was a captive of his lifestyle. He could not let go and follow Christ. He was frozen to his assets. When Jesus cut through his self-justifying morality, the man's confidence in himself and the material strength of his world was shaken.

He had been led to believe that his wealth was a testimony to his goodness. After all, had not God blessed His people in the past? God had always cared for His creation, feeding the sparrows of the air, putting colorful garments on the wildflowers in the meadows.

Jesus Himself reemphasized the providence of God to the crowds who listened to His sermon on the hillside. Don't be anxious, He told them. Don't worry about where your next meal will come from, or where you will get clothes to wear. "Your heavenly father knows that you need them all," Jesus assured them (cf. Matthew 6:25-33).

And had not God blessed His faithful people with milk and honey *in abundance* so that on the surface it appears a divine privilege to be abundantly wealthy? And to be told to give up his abundance in order to follow Christ would seem to be turning away from the blessing of God.

But such wealth has not always been evidence of the blessing of God. In fact, the accumulation of wealth in the Bible has often been proof of the oppression of the poor. And when this is disguised in a cloak of religion, it becomes bitterly offensive to God.

"The Lord enters into judgment with the elders and princes of his people: 'It is you who have devoured the vineyard, the spoil of the poor is in your houses. What do you mean by crushing my people, by grinding the face of the poor?' says the Lord God of hosts" (Isaiah 3:14, 15; RSV).

"Therefore because you trample upon the poor and take from him exactions of wheat. . . . I hate, I despise your [religious] feasts, and I take no delight in your solemn assemblies. Even though you offer me your burnt offerings and cereal offerings, I will not accept them. . . . But let justice roll down like waters, and righteousness like an everflowing stream" (Amos 5:11, 21, 22, 24; RSV).

Consider the accusation from minorities that North American justice is weighted in favor of the wealthy. Is it accurate to draw this conclusion from the greater numbers of minorities in our prisons? What other arguments might support or weaken the charge?

In North America it is undeniably true that God has blessed us abundantly beyond even the splendor of King Solomon. Yet even Solomon's glory was of the world, dependent on heavy taxes and forced labor.

> What happened after King Solomon died? What was the major reason given by the people for the events that happened? See 1 Kings 12:7-16. Was there another contributing factor? See 1 Kings 11:1-13.

If it is true that our abundance in part comes at the expense of the poor in other nations, then it has nothing to do with God's blessing and may actually be hastening our moral and spiritual judgment.

There is no doubting that Christians share in the affluence of this economic advantage. And as Christians, insofar as we do not deliberately seek to live in contrast to that affluent advantage, we are responsible for the worsening condition of the world's poor.

The question is, what can we do? If we send them wheat, we undermine their initiative. Yet if we do not buy their products competitively we won't be able to afford them at all. And if we all go back to locusts and wild honey the economy of the world will collapse.

Yet to continue as we are with no serious attempt to deal with our affluent advantage is to risk the judgment of the rest of the world, if not of God.

Let's explore a direction for us to take as seemingly helpless individuals in attacking the darkness which looms in front of us. It is a possible course of action which will help us to cope in a fruitful way with world problems including spiritual as well as ecological and economic "walls of separation." For if we are to be realistic, the human condition remains unchanged until the spiritual separation is healed. The affluent ignorer-of-God may be more comfortable than his poverty-stricken counterpart, but he is no closer to the salvation and fulfilment which God has freely provided.

Here then are the three steps which we believe will move us in the direction of God's lifestyle for mission which will be developed further in Parts II and III of the book:

Step one: Begin with a personal evaluation of what we are living for, with the aim of discovering and turning over to God those personal gifts and talents which may have gone unused in serving God and His creation. Expect help in this from one another in our congregations and in the larger church.

Step two: Deliberately work toward the personal discovery and expression of a simplified servant style of life. Cut loose from our dependency on the mammon of consumer economics so as to be freely available to the Spirit of God. He may have something new to tell us of ways we can light a candle rather than curse the darkness.

Step three: Put ourselves and our developing gifts fully at the disposal of Christ in His kingdom. Not just as an usher or Sunday school helper but in vocation as well as avocation, a total person totally available in Christ.

As individuals we may not exercise a great deal of leverage even in an individualistic-oriented world. But Christ works collectively. And He can add together all the collective gifts of His people into His own combination of effective mission. We are fitly joined together for this purpose in one body, which is Christ's, led by the one Spirit which He gives us as our guide.

Borrowing from Paul's letter to the Ephesian Christians, we can encourage one another to lead lives appropriate to the calling to which we have been called, "Be always humble, gentle, and patient. Show your love by being tolerant with one another. Do your best to preserve the unity which the Spirit gives by means of the peace that binds you together. There is one body and one Spirit, just as there is one hope to which God has called you. . . .

"It was he who 'gave gifts to mankind'; he appointed some to be apostles, others to be prophets, others to be evangelists, others to be pastors and teachers. He did this to prepare all God's people for the work of Christian service, in order to build up the body of Christ. And so we shall all come together to that oneness in our faith and in our knowledge of the Son of God; we shall become mature people, reaching to the very height of Christ's full stature" (Ephesians 4:2-4, 11-13, GNB).

The process is deceptively simple. We give ourselves to Christ and His church. He equips His church with the organization, the teaching, the resources so that we are enabled—each one of us—to become all that we can be, fully developing and exercising our gifts and abilities. Then Christ fits us together in a totality, a completeness that is His presence in our time. It is only together through our unity in Christ and His kingdom that His love and righteousness and peace can conquer the "principalities and dark powers and wickedness in high places" (Ephesians 6:12) which is so evident from our present world's frightful condition.

Finally: for too long we have shared willingly in an economic upper hand which has given us unfair advantage over the "have-nots." Until our lifestyles begin to show that we reject that advantage, we will continue to be part of the oppressive problem for the world's poor. Furthermore, Jesus calls us to be the freeing answer.

As we seek out a serving manner of life, we will find we have company. *The people of God are called out together to help each other* to be the reconciling change-agents in His world. We will have to become much more skilled at discovering what our gifts are and how they should be employed as servants of Christ to His world. And our congregations will have a greater educational role than just teaching us what the Bible means for our lives. We will need all the help we can get to uncover our talents, buried under heaps of misdirection and misuse. That is the direction we turn to now in the next section.

By the renewing grace of God we can adapt to God's right way for our lives. Supported by the body of Christ and led by His Spirit, we can demonstrate a new kind of lifestyle to the world.

Transition
From—Where is our affluent lifestyle leading us?

Imagine that you are a member of a poor peasant family in Pakistan, with little land and few possessions. How would you expect to provide for your family? With your present education, consider what plans you might make to break the poverty cycle. What resources would you need? What mobility? Preference from authorities?

Now estimate your ability to plan and make the necessary changes if you had a much more restricted education and awareness of resources than you have now.

What might you believe about North Americans? Why? Where would North American Christians fit in your perceptions? How might you look at Christian missions? What might you think of Christianity as compared to your local religion? How would you see local Christians?

To—Part II, Chapter 4, Becoming all we can be

We are accustomed to think that answers to world problems are a responsibility of world governments. We forget that the course of history has been altered by the thoughts and actions of individuals.

So the first step to changing our world is to allow God to work a change in us. We are designed by God to become like Him in responsibility for ourselves and for those whom our lives can touch.

In Chapter 4 we will take a first look at the potential for us in uncovering our talents and discovering our gifts. And what that might mean in terms of fulfillment for us individually and for our place in the body of Christ, His church. See Luke 19:1-10.

Part II, Chapter 4—Becoming all we can be

A. The frustrations of unused abilities.

B. The joys of channeled abilities.
   1. Process of talent discovery illustrated.
   2. Need for fulfillment and belonging is a strong drive.
   3. Jesus converts Zacchaeus' work life (Luke 19:1-10).
   4. Jesus, the blueprint for our lives.

Part II

The Potential of Power:
Personal Talents in Mission

4
Becoming all we can be

Now let us play hide and seek. Should you hide in my heart it would not be difficult to find you. But should you hide behind your own shell, then it would be useless for anyone to seek you.

—Kahlil Gibran in *Sand and Foam*

"If Mennonites would get the baptism of the Holy Ghost, they could become a real witness in the world," Carl insists. "As it is, we're too weak and losing out to the world."

To prove his point, he documents how unsuccessful his congregation has been at winning their neighbors to Christ.

"Our congregation is barely holding its own. We haven't had a new adult member from the world for 10-15 years."

When Carl talks like this in his Sunday school class, he creates both irritation and interest. His pastor gives him some support because he believes Carl is partly right, but for partly the wrong reasons.

While some members of Carl's class appreciate the vigorous faith and witness of charismatic Christians, others resent being pigeonholed as "Spirit-less" because they do not speak in tongues or experience faith healing. But even these will admit to being impressed with the spiritual achievements of the charismatic movement. And some will even confess to a desire for a more effectual ministry in their lives.

And in this they are like Carl and many others who have sought the charismatic experience. Unwilling to continue to suffer inactivity and ineffectiveness in their Christian lives, they seek a breakthrough of power, "Holy Ghost power," in order to bypass the blocks to service they have felt in their lives.

For some, the frustrated search is pursued until tongues and other gifts of the Spirit are experienced. And the new fellowship with others who share similar experiences becomes a joy and delight. Frustrations are forgotten. Those on the outside are eagerly invited to join in.

But for others, the frustrations may rise again. In fact, an increased appreciation for the power of God may only heighten a sense of inadequacy when the Christian finds himself unable to release that power or Presence in appropriate service to the world.

And too often his church hasn't helped. "Service" has meant a meeting in a building, not to serve but to sit. He may be asked to be an usher, or teach a class—if he's been around long enough to absorb the doctrines deemed necessary to be reinforced in his teaching.

He is encouraged to participate in the selected routines which are felt to develop unity in the group. If he fails in this and withdraws he is judged not to have the right spirit, or even to have the Spirit at all—but no one questions the routines. Or the level of fellowship. Thank God if he turns to the charismatic movement. Others like him may simply fade from the scene altogether and scarcely be missed.

Evaluate your experience by checking the most appropriate completing word: I am asked to serve the church in ways that suit my abilities____ frequently, ____ sometimes, ____ rarely, ____ never. The other members in our congregation are given opportunity to serve Christ with their individual gifts ____ frequently, ____ sometimes, ____ rarely, ____ never.

But let's dream of yet another possibility for the church in its biblical approach to service which would make use of the total lifestyle of each member.

In two years Phyllis and Joel have grown from visitors to enthusiastic members of a Mennonite congregation near their home. Their initial visit followed upon the suggestion of one of Phyllis' acquaintances at work.

It has been a remarkable experience for them both, because the congregation has demonstrated an intense interest in all that they are, including the "secular" work they perform in the community. In fact, Phyllis has changed jobs recently with the encouragement and help of her Talent Group at the church (whose purpose is to uncover talents and encourage their use). They discovered she would enjoy the opportunity offered by another department in the bank where she worked, so she applied.

"Joel and I took the Talent Discovery course they have developed at the church, and I found out a lot about myself," Phyllis explains. "I wasn't sure I'd be good at computer bookkeeping, but the tests I took gave me a lot of confidence."

The course also confirmed Joel's mechanical skills and that he would likely continue to enjoy his job in the auto-body shop where he is employed.

But the most exciting thing about the course for both

of them lay in the discovery that they are both doing what God wants them to do. And that their jobs are a vital part of the mission of the congregation in serving their community.

"Before, I always felt vaguely guilty I wasn't a missionary or something," Joel says. "Where we used to live, it seemed all the church wanted was for us to show up a couple times a week, and bring our money.

"Sure, we'd heard sermons and Sunday school lessons on being good Christians wherever we worked. But this is different!"

How different it is shows up in the kinds of questions their Talent Group asks about their work. On her first report night, Phyllis told the group what she did, who she worked with, who she talked with on her lunch breaks. Then the questions came.

"Which of the other employees looks as if she needs you as a friend?" "Has God given you an indication of what He wants you to do when your supervisor pushes more of the other girls' work on you?" "Is your schedule and Joel's letting you enjoy each other the way you'd like to?"

"It's as if our church is really interested in who I am," Phyllis confides. "Because really, we are what we do. And with their interest in helping me be a full-time Christian where I work, then I feel like it's important. And that I'm really in the bank for a purpose."

Phyllis and Joel were commissioned by the congregation in a special ceremony with two other couples one Sunday morning. Their Talent Group laid hands on their heads and shoulders while the congregation read:

"Your special responsibility in the body of Christ is acknowledged by us as your service for our Lord. You are

God's representatives and a part of us where you work and live. We thank God for you and the privileges you have in Christ. Serve Him well among those to whom He sends you with His love."

Joel and Phyllis and each member of this envisioned congregation look upon what they do through the week as their major responsibility in the church, both in vocations and avocations. Consequently the times they spend together in the congregation focus mainly on helping each other achieve the growth God calls each one to attain in their lives. They believe in this way they can achieve their optimum strength as a group, together and in the community.

They do not study the Bible for itself, but for the specific direction and help each person needs in his or her situation. They help each other set personal goals in their vocations and avocations as the bench marks of God's leading. But they have learned not to be judgmental of anyone's progress. "After all, who are you to criticize the servant of somebody else, especially when that somebody else is God?" (Romans 14:4, Phillips).

Consider the most recent members joining your congregation. How many are children of members? How many are transfers from other congregations? People from the community? How much do you know about their work? Their interests?

"Naturally there are different gifts and functions; individually grace is given to us in different ways out of the rich diversity of Christ's giving. . . . His gifts were made that Christians might be properly equipped for their service, that the whole body might be built up until the time comes when, in the unity of common faith and com-

mon knowledge of the Son of God, we arrive at real
maturity—that measure of development which is meant
by 'the fullness of Christ' " (Ephesians 4:7, 12, 13,
Phillips).

Why do people join the church today? Perhaps because there is nowhere else to turn. Some people are so
desperate for an answer to their lives that they will ex-
pose themselves to the totally different and often bizarre
experience which is "church."

Because on the surface, "church" is like nothing else
in the life of the community. The newcomer will sit for
an hour without the opportunity to switch to another
channel. He will be asked to give money to help pay for
buildings and facilities he or his family may use only a
couple of hours a week—and that not for bowling or
swimming or union meetings. In fact, he may even find
his participation in such groups or activities are not approved.

If the climate he meets demands so much and gives
only promises of spiritual love and fellowship in return
how great must be his desperation if he persists? Truly he
must fight his way into such a kingdom.

But suppose the climate in the congregation is one of
concern for all that the person may become by the grace
of God. If the chalice of God which is so offered is full of
interest in what he is and help for what he may become
in both vocation and avocation, how much more likely he
is to drink from such a heartwarming cup!

The need for fulfillment and belonging are strong
drives in every one of us. Even the most sin-possessed
knows a desire to grow toward maturity, distorted as that
maturity is perceived to be. Given the chance to feel welcome, allowed to hope for creative help in maturing,

warmed with a sense of belonging, many more persons may thread the narrow gate onto the straight way which leads to the fullness of Christ.

In the church we have expected the world to come to us, to our Sunday schools and evangelistic programs. We have developed bus ministries and day-care programs to capture their interest. We train evangelistic teams to go out in visitation. We encourage neighborhood Bible studies and long for the good old days when people responded to these techniques.

But "techniques" only work on the few who will accept such manipulation. And the masses pass us by because we do not touch (so they think) the real issues of their lives. "Believe in the Lord Jesus Christ and thou shalt be saved" is terribly real to us. But it may be totally unreal for the woman who is being torn apart in an ongoing conflict with her husband. She needs the gospel translated into terms which can cope with the mind-numbing agonies of her everyday situation.

So also with the man or woman on a routine job. The work may have some meaning in profits or service, but only as a cog serves the wheel, or the card feeds the computer. So the gospel must be translated into workday terms that can bring purpose and meaning to life.

And today the children of the church need meaning in the gospel too. Our preaching and teaching can be pointless to our sons and daughters if we aren't interesting them in a lifestyle which can free them to face the awesome problems of the future. Their future.

It is not enough to teach and preach although these are essential. Only those with some capacity for introspection can make the transfer from ideal to real.

Jesus dealt in the real. He exampled the meaning of

faith in physical terms. Zacchaeus was chief tax collector in the Jericho district. When Jesus came to Jericho, Zacchaeus showed his desperate desire for some change in his life by shedding his dignity and climbing a tree to get a look at Jesus—the Man whose life was so different from his own. (See Luke 19:1-10.)

Now Zacchaeus' problems were not the same as those of the blind and the lame. For them Jesus spoke the immediate freeing word and broke their chains of physical bondage. But Zacchaeus had a moral and ethical problem and would need the good word from Jesus in a different way. He would need another challenge than that given to the paralytic, "Take up your bed and walk."

Jesus didn't explain ethical principles or biblical teaching to Zacchaeus. Instead he chose to deal with the tax man's lifestyle.

"I must come and stay with you today," Jesus told Zacchaeus. Standing with them on the dusty road were the everyday people who had paid a heavy tax-plus-commission to this puppet of the Romans. And Jesus asked to see his house! See the luxury of his lifestyle made possible by the very people who stood around them.

The reality of Jesus and His life made Zacchaeus' own life vividly clear in that moment. Little wonder that the first thing Zacchaeus said was, "Here and now, Lord, I give half my possessions to the poor, and if I have defrauded anyone, I will repay him four times over."

For Zacchaeus a new sense of purpose is unfolding here, a new direction for living. And for the doubting crowd here is demonstrable evidence of the reality of the kingdom of God, as Jesus points out, "Today salvation has come to this house."

Helping each one of us to become all we can be is the

mission of the church so that together we can be the responsible people of God He has meant us to be. The blueprint for our lives is Jesus Christ. If we can demonstrate this mission in practical, meaningful applications for the vocations and avocations of each other's lives, we will capture the vital interest of the world around us.

Transition
From—Becoming all we can be

At this point it is important to know the real value of the church of Christ, both to you and to the world. How much moral wholesomeness does your community owe to the collective example of the people of God? How might your community live today if it were left to the people who do not now live as followers of Christ?

Which of the teachings of Jesus would improve the environment where you work? (For instance, in the Sermon on the Mount, Matthew 5—7). How might your own attitudes change if you were supported like Phyllis and Joel in living the Christlike way at your work?

To—Chapter 5, Discovering talents, discerning gifts

Many of us have not used our abilities and interests for so long—if ever—that we hardly know what they are. So we live distorted lives, pursuing diversions rather than fulfillment.

Abilities sparked with Spirit-led interest is a working definition of the biblical term *talent*. Here are practical steps to take in uncovering buried talents by evaluating (1) past activities, (2) present feelings about possible vocations and avocations, and (3) future requirements which may have to be met.

The process will take on the character of God when (1) we make it a matter of continual prayer, (2) we seek others' counsel, (3) submit our thinking to the Bible, (4) test our gifts, (5) measure our activities by the love of God, and (6) submit ourselves and our talents to the body of Christ, the church.

In Chapter 5 our objective then is to develop some skills for uncovering our talents and verifying their God-given validity. Matthew 24 and 25, 1 Corinthians 12.

Chapter 5—Discovering talents, discerning gifts

A. Basics of talents and gifts.
    1. Biblical concept of talent-gifts (Matthew 25:14-30).
    2. Biblical purpose of talent-gifts (Matthew 25:31-46)

B. Methods to discover talents, gifts, abilities, and interests.
    1. Local resources.
    2. Do-it-yourself program.
        a. Explore your past.
        b. Consider present feelings.
        c. Anticipate future possibilities.
    3. Process of focusing your talent-gifts.
        a. Pray continually about it.
        b. Seek counsel of others.
        c. Submit thinking to the Bible.
        d. Try your gifts by faith.
        e. Expect gifts to express love of God.
        f. Submit yourself and gifts to the church (1 Corinthians 12:12-25).

5
Discovering talents, discerning gifts

Some people say the hardest work you will ever have to do is the job of getting a job. After all, it involves divining who you are, what you want, and where you are going with your life. . . .

Impatience, the desire to get it over with, fast, can cost you and your loved one (or ones) many thousands of dollars over the next decade or two, as well as condemn you to a fruitless occupation in which you continually feel under-valued, misused and miserable. . . .

And the irony of all this is: considering the present chaotic mess that the national "job market" is, it can take you just as long to get a poor job which pays much less and ignores the talents God gave you, as it can take you to get a good job.
—Richard Nelson Bolles in *What Color Is Your Parachute?*

What are "talents" and "gifts"? According to dictionary definitions, a talent seems to be a natural ability or power, a natural endowment which can be developed and enhanced with practice.

A gift suggests a bestowed ability, a gift you have received rather than developed through cultivation or practice. In the church we have made much of the distinctions between natural talents and spiritual gifts.

But the distinctions may not be too important. In the parable of Jesus—from which we get the term "talent"—

the three servants are *given* the talents by their master. So that talents as Jesus used the term are gifts too (see Matthew 25:14-30).

What we do with our talents and gifts is vital to us. In the parable, the man who buried his talent for fear of losing it also lost his place in his master's light. But the servants who put their talents to work were commended and rewarded. And that seems to be the substance of the parable—if it is taken by itself.

But Jesus does not tell this story by itself. He has been responding to an earlier question from His disciples about the end of the world (see Matthew 24:3). And Jesus paints a vivid picture of how God will evaluate those who profess to believe and serve Him. So the parable of the talents is only a part of Jesus' answer.

As He begins to respond, Jesus says that the end of this age will be marked with confusion: false messiahs offering to save the world, and times of great tribulation and terrible signs in the heavens. However, people will live as if these evidences of the abnormal were normal. And so they will not live a prepared-for-anything life. Yet as Jesus points out, being prepared is important because not even He knows the day and the hour when our world will collapse around us.

So Jesus describes the wise servant (Matthew 24:45 ff.) as one who is always ready for the return of his master. He is one who isn't diverted by appeals to the long-delayed return of Christ, but lives in available anticipation. In contrast, the superficial person (like the foolish bridesmaids of Matthew 25:1-13) will miss the occasion through lack of foresight.

At this point Jesus tells the parable of the talents. All that has gone before describes the kind of person who is aware of the world's condition, can discern the false from the real, and is alert to the leading of God. Now, the given talents are put to work vigorously for the purposes of God—but what purposes? And how are the talents to be used?

In the final parable of judgment (Matthew 25:31-46) Jesus sums up the lifestyle of the person who is responsibly alive, who puts all that he or she is becoming at the service of others in need. For that is serving Christ. Feeding the hungry. Giving those who thirst for the right way a drink of living water. Being helpfully hospitable to those who find their world strange and frightening. Clothing those who stand naked of resources. Visiting the sick and sick at heart. Sitting with the prisoners behind the bars of injustice and oppression.

"And the King will point out, 'I tell you, whatever you did for the most humble of these my brethren, you did it for me' " (Matthew 25:40).

> Evaluate the way you are now living in the light of Jesus' statement, "I was hungry and you gave me food . . . naked and you clothed me, I was sick and you visited me." Does this represent your activities ____ usually, ____ sometimes, ____ rarely, ____ never?

Unfortunately many of us find it difficult to know what our gifts and talents are. How do we find out what we have been given to use in service to others? Remember, we are what we do. So it is important to do what we are.

For young people, there are batteries of helpful tests offered by high schools. Guidance counselors should be helpful resources for youth (and for parents who want to help) in finding some avenues to explore.

For exploration is the norm. Unfortunately it is almost easier for someone else to pinpoint our talents, abilities, or gifts than it is for us to do so ourselves.

Here is where the church should fit in, because there is much more to the talent search than taking a battery of psychological tests.

But let's start with the tests and the church. If the local congregation really wants to become effective in its mission, it will take up the responsibility of helping each one of its adult members (and adherents) to discover their talents and discern their gifts.

The congregation can find a variety of tests and resources at their local community college. The community college system is designed not only for youth but for continuing education of older adults as well. (See Chapter 6 and the Appendix for a list of commonly available texts and tests.) Some other colleges who have continuing education programs may have similar resources.

Also most large cities have professional career counseling services—for a price. A congregation may be able to negotiate an acceptable testing arrangement with such a service for considerably less than private counseling might cost.

What about do-it-yourself programs? Psychologist Joyce Brothers outlines an interesting do-it-yourself plan in her book, *The Brothers System for Liberated Love and Marriage* (New York: Peter W. Wyden, Inc., 1972).

She suggests that you write down the five things you want to do more than anything else. This is more difficult to do than it seems initially. Most of us think in terms of duties or peer practices. We choose to list what others expect of us rather than our own deepest interests.

Yet we need to discover the deep-seated interests that may have been submerged in doing the expected: "going to school" or "settling down." Or even "serving the Lord," where this is a narrowly defined set of functions such as teaching a Bible class or going into Voluntary Service for two years.

Consider this: the mission of your life is the unique combination of one or more basic abilities or gifts pulled together by an interest awakened in you by the presence of God. Deep-seated interests may be closer to the person God would produce in us than the person we have allowed ourselves to be, because the interests may be the clue, not only to the shape of our talents or gifts, but how the Spirit of Christ would lead us to express these in serving His church and His world.

So self-evaluation of your most significant interests can help you find not only your major abilities and gifts but also how they can be worked out in a fulfilling lifestyle.

So take the assignment seriously. Make a list of the five or more things you want to do in the years ahead. At this stage don't get caught in the pitfall of whether you can accomplish your dreams—save that for later.

Explore your past. Reach back into the different stages and times of your life for the experiences which you enjoyed—and those which were disappointing. Use these to guide you in identifying clearly the activities which interest you. And, for a check, those which definitely disinterest you.

Consider your present feelings about a variety of activities around you: hobbies, politics, creative work, passing knowledge on to others, digging out information, working with your hands, helping people with problems, using words and language, athletic challenges, music or art, supervising others, working with committees, selling products or services, communicating ideas, working with machinery, thinking through abstract concepts, exploring numbers, organizing a system.

Think of people you know, the work they do, and the hobbies they enjoy. How you feel about the many activities you see around you will help you to sift out the few you are most interested in doing.

Cluster the interests in the groups which seem to go together. And keep ranking the groups—this one comes out on top, that one is less interesting and sinks to the bottom.

Anticipate future possibilities for the interests which seem to be emerging as your God-given talents. Will you need further training? Are they things you can do in your present location? How will your family be affected? Will you need to combine one or more activities in order to earn a living? (A later chapter on earning will help put this in perspective.)

> For further study: Expand your talent search with a historical diary. Try to recall each year of your life in order to remember the interests you held—or which held you—at that time. Carry it up through the present.

Think about your list every day over a number of weeks, even months. Keep working at it. Add to your clusters as other important interests come to your mind. Drop all but the five or six most vital ones. Keep refining your list as you check it out in the following six processes:

1. *Pray about it continually.* Prayer is not only a specific act when requests are verbalized to God. Prayer is also the openhearted desire to live always in communication with the Spirit of Christ.

It is the possibility Jesus promised to His followers in John 14:23 and 26, "Anyone who loves me will heed what I say; then my Father will love him, and we will come to him and make our dwelling with him. . . . The Advocate, the Holy Spirit whom the Father will send in my name, will teach you everything, and will call to mind all that I have told you" (NEB).

2. *Seek the counsel of others.* Here is where the church can help you—that is, if it takes its responsibility in the body of Christ seriously. Some congregations have mid-week meetings and small-group fellowships where counsel can be asked for and received.

Ask members of your family and your friends: "What do you think I could best do with my life? In your opinion, what are my gifts and abilities?" Put their suggestions on your list. They may well see in you gifts that you have overlooked.

3. *Submit your thinking to the Bible.* Read large chunks of the Bible for help in seeing yourself as God sees you. Pay attention to Jesus in the Gospels. Study Romans. Get a good modern translation to help you with the Old Testament, especially the prophets Isaiah and Amos.

4. *Try your gifts by faith.* You won't need to change your vocation in order to test the possibilities of your interests and talents. Experiment by faith. Do some work in the area of your interests to see how your talents emerge.

Then expect God to give you some definite indications to confirm you in your gifts. Don't expect applause. Instead look for a beginning sense of satisfaction and peace of mind, and the affirmation of the fellowship of faith. Look for these spiritual evidences of direction even if your experiments in faith end in frustrating failure, because frustration and failure may only mean a misapplication of your gifts. Try again!

5. *Expect your gifts to express the love of God.* This is more sure than your feelings, because feelings can often confuse. The gifts of God will find a way to serve His love to the world—unless you bury them! *Here is the meaning of your life—to put all that you are to work as the unique gift of God for building His kingdom in your particular place and time.*

No one else can fill your shoes or take up your potential in the movement of God. Only you have been given the unique combination of gifts and acquaintances, interests and environment, talents and people to love them by.

So an integral part of your personal talent search is to rediscover the particular people you are given to love—family, friends, work mates, neighbors—the infirm, imprisoned, and oppressed. They may not always be as lovable as you may want, but that's all right. None of us are as lovable as we think we are. And if God has a unique gift of people for you to love—He will give you the love you need. As long as you don't bury it too!

6. *Submit yourself and your talents-gifts to the church.* All that you are in faith is part of the presence of God in the world today. Together with the people of God you form the body of Christ. In consequence, your talents are multiplied and reinforced as they fit together in Christ.

As the Apostle Paul wrote, "For Christ is like a single body with its many limbs and organs, which, many as they are, together make up one body. . . . In fact, God appointed each limb and organ to its own place in the body, as he chose. If the whole were one single organ, there would not be a body at all; in fact, however, there are many different organs, but one body. The eye cannot say to the hand, 'I do not need you'; nor the head to the feet, 'I do not need you. . . .' But God has combined the various parts of the body, giving special honour to the humbler parts, so that there might be no sense of division in the body, but that all its organs might feel the same concern for one another" (1 Corinthians 12:12, 18-21, 24, 25, NEB).

Jesus said, "I am the vine, and you the branches. He who dwells in me, as I dwell in him, bears much fruit; for apart from me you can do nothing" (John 15:5, NEB).

Your gifts and abilities will find their value—and fulfillment—as part of the living presence of God in your world today.

Transition

From—Discovering talents, discerning gifts

The more seriously you pursue your talent search, the more thoroughly you will understand yourself and your interests. Ask yourself—how close am I now to fulfilling what God has given to me to benefit His world and His people?

Some people are so unaccustomed to self-evaluation that they will tire quickly with the unexpected effort. Others busy themselves in self-condemnation continually. Where do you find yourself? Self-evaluation can free you from self-condemnation by helping you to appreciate God's gifts, to you and through you.

To—Chapter 6, What the church can do for you

The world shapes our working lives as much as or more than the church. But with creative planning the local congregation can draw together the resources to help every member determine God's leading for their vocations and avocations. Books for individual and group study, testing devices, and counseling services can form a flexible response to each member's needs.

In Chapter 6, we will shift our view of the major ministry of the congregation to developing the ministry of the members. The congregation has a responsibility to move from self-interest ("keeping the wheels turning") to developing the ministries in which their members *can serve God in His world.* The meaning of membership and fellowship then takes on new dimensions. See Acts 2:42-47; Titus 2:1-13; 3:8.

Chapter 6—What the church can do for you

A. Church responsibility for lifestyle planning.
    1. Abdicated responsibility to the world.
    2. Responsibility recovered through action.
        a. Passive resources available.
            i. Notable books.
            ii. Notable tests.
        b. Active resources possible.
            i. Leadership team.
            ii. Small groups or classes.

B. Life together in the congregation.
    1. Not measured by numbers.
    2. God's grace disciplines our lives (Titus 2:1-13; 3:8).
    3. Purpose: to reach others (illustrated) (Acts 2:42-47).
    4. Contrasted to other world systems.

6

What the church can do for you

The measure of failure on the part of the church is the measure in which she has allowed herself to be influenced by the spirit of the age, because she has been untrue to the facts of her own life. We are sometimes told today that what the church supremely needs is that she should catch the spirit of the age. A thousand times no. What the church supremely needs is to correct the spirit of the age. . . .

The church of God needs no new visitation of power from God. She needs the realization of the power she already has, the appropriation of the forces already resident within her.
—G. Campbell Morgan in *Living Messages*

Each congregation should take seriously its primary responsibility to be the major source of counsel and guidance for every member's lifestyle planning.

Teaching the Bible is important. But the objective of that teaching is to make disciples. That is our primary responsibility.

However, too often we have allowed the world to shape our disciples instead. We have exercised little or no influence on the career selection of fellow members in our congregations. We concern ourselves mainly with the voluntary skills of those who keep our congregational wheels turning. Or the fewer still who choose full-time service as church workers.

But all of us are in full-time service. Or at least God intends us to be. Why then are most of us in jobs we backed into rather than ones we chose in good stewardship? It is estimated that 80 percent of North America's working force are now employed at jobs below their capabilities. The result is frustrated potential and apathy during what should be our most effective hours of the week. Further, we display an excessive dependence upon "leisure time" to find purpose and meaning in life.

William Elster heads up Studies for Urban Man, Inc., in Tempe, Arizona. In his system for vocational exploration he points to the terrible waste of our human resources.

"It is ironic," Elster states, "in a society which values work so highly that often more energy and care is expended in choosing clothes or an automobile than in choosing a lifework.

"The result is that many people do not choose their work at all. They happen by merest accident of time and place to fall into a given occupational field."

How did you choose your vocation, ____trained for it at school, ____parents' influence, ____ friend's influence, ____ only job available, ____ wanted to do it.

So in the search for talents and interest-abilities the individual must not be abandoned to go it alone. There is no reason why congregational structures cannot be adapted or reorganized to provide needed encouragement and resources.

On the passive level of resources, church libraries could add several copies of *What Color Is Your Parachute?* by Richard Nelson Bolles (Berkeley, Calif.: Ten Speed Press, 1972). In 1969 Bolles was commissioned by

United Ministries in Higher Education (a coalition of ten major Protestant denominations) to explore the field of occupational decision-making. The result is his book, acknowledged by many professionals as the most helpful single resource for lifestyle planning now extant. It is enjoyably easy to read.

An outstanding resource for small groups is based on Bolles' book and is designed as a practical workbook for career and life planning: *Where Do I Go from Here with My Life?* by John C. Crystal and Richard N. Bolles. It is available from Seabury Press in New York.

An excellent series of self-studies especially for women who wish to combine family responsibilities and a career is produced by *Catalyst*, 6 East 82nd Street, New York, NY 10028.

The United Methodists have developed their *Time and Talent Program* as a means to "enable all members to respond joyously to church-related responsibilities with their talent level" and to develop and release every member's talent. The program is designed first to get each member involved in self-assessment for service in the congregation. It has an innovative file card system for listing available talent for all phases of congregational activity.

There are many sources of testing devices available but few as generally helpful as the Hall Occupational Orientation Inventory (Scholastic Testing Service, Inc., 480 Meyer Road, Bensenville, IL 60106). There are 220 statements which the person evaluates on a scale from most desirable to very undesirable. The forms provided allow for immediate self-interpretation. The scoring helps to analyze psychological needs, worker traits, and job characteristics in 22 areas such as creativity, risk, security, belongingness, esteem, satisfaction, data-things-people orientation, and concerns for location, aptitude, physical abilities, co-workers, environment, and financial reward.

Actively, the leadership team in the congregation should be expanded to include life-planning counsel as a major function of pastoral ministries. The value of this ministry will increase directly with success in helping each member find his or her mission-fulfilling situation.

Further, small groups or classes can be formed in the congregation with the help of one or more of the resources mentioned above. The goal of all these ministries is to help both youths and adults find *their* ministry in the world.

> Take a survey: Of the resources listed above, which would you prefer to use? _____ book for individual study, _____group study, _____pastoral team member for counsel, _____ individual testing devices.

The local congregation as an employment agency? Why not? If as part of its mission to the world the local congregation finds meaningful employment for its people, and helps retrain those who seek more fruitful employment, we could experience a new examination of the good news by the world. For then the good news would have moved closer to the needs and hurts—and the hopes—of the people.

And if such employment (paid or unpaid) is perceived as part of the total lifestyle of the people of God, then the love and fellowship of the congregation will have been demonstrated unmistakably. "By this," Jesus told His followers, "all men will know that you are my disciples, if you have love for one another" (John 13:35, RSV).

Unfortunately, many congregations today are self-serving, cannibalizing the flock of God rather than feeding it.

In the cannibal church, members are devoured to keep the organization alive. People are used for the sake of the structure. Discipline becomes a set of rules by which to measure one another in order to purify the church, rather than to help one another develop in Christ.

It is to the continuing shame of the cannibal church that it processes people into its own graven image, rather than freeing and enabling them to grow in the image of Christ.

Where is the cannibal church found? Wherever its members are thought of only as potential ushers or church school teachers or finance committee members. Wherever complaints are heard that members aren't showing up at midweek meetings. Or aren't supporting the annual revival services.

But the church is not meetings to attend or numbers to count. It is people being helped to eat of the bread of life.

The Apostle Paul doesn't ask Timothy how his building program is going. Nor does he complain to Titus that his people aren't buying official church material. No, in the church of Christ things exist for people, not the other way around.

In his letters to Titus and Timothy, Paul lays out an idealized lifestyle for their congregations. He describes what he expects of congregational leaders and of the lives of the Christians in their care. They should live simply, cleanly, and joyously.

"For the grace of God has dawned upon the world with healing for all mankind; and by it we are disciplined to renounce godless ways and worldly desires, and to live a life of temperance, honesty, and godliness in the present age, looking forward to the happy fulfilment of our hope when the splendour of our great God and Saviour Christ Jesus will appear. . . .

"Those who have come to believe in God should see that they engage in honourable occupations, which are not only honourable in themselves, but also useful to their fellow-men" (Titus 2:11-13; 3:8; NEB).

The work of the church isn't to keep its wheels turning. Instead, as Paul urges Timothy, "First, supplications, prayers, intercessions and thanksgiving should be made on behalf of all men: for kings and rulers in positions of responsibility, so that our common life may be lived in peace and quiet, *with a proper sense of God and of our responsibility to him for what we do with our lives.* In the sight of God our Savior this is undoubtedly the right thing to pray for; for his purpose is that all men should be saved and come to realize the truth" (1 Timothy 2:1-4, Phillips, italics mine).

> Which statement most accurately describes your congregation? _____ cares more about what its members do in their work, _____ cares more about how its members can serve the church, _____ cares equally for its members' vocation and their work for the church.

Life together in a congregation is a result of God's initiative in grace. Or at least it is meant to be. God's expressed desire for the humanity He created is to encourage every one of us to experience fullness of life within His kingdom, despite our preoccupation with all that is less than life around us.

Yet unfortunately that is our style. Humanity busies itself with low-level survival, clutching and struggling for ego position like racehorses out of a starting gate.

Pride of life is the biblical expression for it. We love the world of our own creation, with all its potential for status and power. Yet that exciting, tantalizing life is death to us. Its glittering light means darkness of spirit. The love it gives is fickle and heartbreaking.

Now the people who do make the choice of God's lifestyle instead of the world's stand out like a new light on a dark street. At least (again) they are meant to do so. God's purpose for His people has always been to light a path so others can find their way out of the lonely darkness.

And most of us have experienced the dark loneliness of the world. One-upmanship, aggression, and the drive to succeed all tend to alienate us one from another. We push each other into pigeonholes, joining in admiration of the strong while climbing over the downtrodden and the meek.

Anne is an example of the meek. An attractive 25-year-old Texan, she is a gentle victim of our world's current educational pigeonholing. Anne would make a fine licensed practical nurse, but somewhere along the line she became persuaded to train for a teaching career. There's nothing the matter with Anne's compassion levels and she would relate well to children—but she carried a C grade.

When she graduated, there were too many A and B level grads competing in the area teachers' job market. So Anne is shoveling french fries and wrapping quarter pounders at McDonalds now. The disappointment and confusion she is experiencing have cut large chunks out of her personality that only Jesus Christ will be able to heal.

And that is why God has given Anne into a community of His people recently. Without hope of a teaching job, unable to even think about retraining as a practical nurse until she gets some debts paid, unwilling to be a continuing burden on her parents who have other children in the educational pipeline, Anne moved to where she could find a job. Any job. And in the months which followed, her confusion and alienation deepened in acute loneliness.

Until a dim memory—a glimpse of the lifestyle of God in her grandfather's stability of faith—came rushing back in the patient joy of a girl who lived in the same rooming house. And she began to go to church with her new friend. It was the opening up of hope again for Anne, hearing reality again when all the world about her seemed to speak in advertising slogans. So every Sunday now she carefully bundles up her soul and her spirit and everything she is—and offers it anew to "*our* Father, who art in heaven. . . ."

"And [the first Christians] . . . met constantly to hear the apostles teach, and to share the common life, to break bread, and to pray. A sense of awe was everywhere, and many marvels and signs were brought about through the apostles. All whose faith had drawn them together held everything in common: they would sell their property and possessions and make a general distribution as the need of each required. With one mind they kept up their daily attendance at the temple, and, breaking bread in private houses, shared their meals with unaffected joy, as they praised God and enjoyed the favour of the whole people. And day by day the Lord added to their number those whom he was saving" (Acts 2:42-47, NEB).

We are not meant to be alone. We are designed to belong in a functioning community of varied peoples, each benefiting from the other, each contributing to the healthy action and interaction of the whole. This isn't a Leninized-Marxist vision of all-*for*-the-state. Nor is it a liberal socialist all-*from*-the-state. Instead, Christian community is meant to show love each for the other, as in the greatest commandment: "Thou shalt love the Lord thy God with all thy heart, and with all thy soul, and with all thy mind. . . . [And] thou shalt love thy neighbour as thyself" (Matthew 22:37, 39, KJV).

Transition
From—What the church can do for you

Now is the time to test the thesis that the major ministry of your congregation should be changed (if it is not doing so now) to developing the Christlike ministries of each member. Does this mean a change in worship programs for your congregation? If so, in what way? What does the Bible suggest to you is the basis of our praise, our appreciation of God's work in our lives?

Or does the church already get too close to our lives in trying to help us? Do we prefer to believe that God instructs us privately in the development of our lifestyles? Yet how much do secular magazines and television programs influence us? For instance, in your experience, did God lead you into your present vocation—or is He helping you to make the best of it, in spite of what you are doing?

To—Chapter 7, What you can do for the church

The failure of the church to consistently demonstrate the love of God is a testimony to the consistency of humankind. But the church is no greater than the faith of its members, faithfully using the gifts of the Spirit. And as demonstrated by Jesus, these gifts can be multiplied to serve the love of God to the world.

Individuals can only give of themselves to the church completely. And this is the objective of Chapter VII, to come to commitment—not only to Christ, but to His church as well.

There is nothing to fear in such a full-scale involvement, for Jesus has reassured us that He will share with us in any demand placed upon us. See Romans 12; 1 Corinthians 12; John 6; Matthew 11:28-30; Galatians 6:2; Ephesians 3:8-10.

Chapter 7—What you can do for the church

A. The church: greater than the sum of its members.
    1. Christians have not always been good examples.
    2. Congregation meant to have visible faith and mutual love.

B. The church depends on its members.
    1. Talent-gifts for work of church (Romans 12; 1 Corinthians 12).
    2. Jesus illustrates to His disciples (John 6).
    3. False arguments against personal involvement.
        a. Takes too much time.
        b. "I will be used superficially."
    4. Submission to Christ and His church.
        a. The burden is light (Matthew 11:28-30).
        b. The burden is shared (Galatians 2:6).
    . Serving together: the church's purpose (Ephesians 3:8-10).

7
What you can do for the church

It is not wise to rank the gifts of the Spirit. All gifts of the Spirit to the church are important. This importance is most noticeable when the gift is absent. When the internal social situation in a congregation is chaotic, probably the most important gift would be found in one able to moderate among the factions and reestablish order. For a floundering church which has lost contact with its historical roots, possibly the most important gift comes in a teacher capable of interpreting its past, helping it to recover its reason for existence in the present, and developing a vision for the future. . . .

The intention of the Holy Spirit is to create community—a community in which the fruits of His ministry are abundantly evident, a community on which the spiritual gifts are poured out to reveal the potential of a church living in anticipation of the coming kingdom already inaugurated by its Lord.

—John Driver in *Community and Commitment*

It must be said at this point that the Christian community has not always succeeded in showing the love of God. In fact, some of history's most profound God-rejectors have done so on account of the distorted view of God they received from the church at that time in that situation. To many historians the rise of atheism in Russia is directly due to the world-likeness of the church there and then. Instead of serving with compassion, the church dominated with power. It had grown hard instead of holy, and its victims were often the poor and the prisoner, the very ones most needing God's caring love.

But that is the nature of humankind, to corrupt the wholesome, to institutionalize charity, to save oneself rather than give oneself to the saving of others. Why should this world-likeness appear in the church, where a clear view of godlikeness should be seen instead? Ah, there is the wonder of it! Faith is so tender a thing it must be totally free of any pressure from God or it is no longer faith. And the faith we have been given to use is only an instrument to grow by, not a magic wand to make us like Christ in one wave.

So the church is no greater than the sum of its faith, no stronger than the weakness of its members. Each congregation has no more going for it than the vitality it can draw from the Christians who give themselves to its life.

And each congregation is meant to have life, a visible body of faith-in-action which clearly expresses what it is like to trust God and follow Him daily in all matters of living. It will be seen in how we ask advice in our decisions. It will show in how we admonish in love the headstrong actions we take so that we don't continue to make the same mistakes again and again.

It will be most visible in how we care for each other, singing together in joy, weeping together in tragedy. For we find meaning and purpose and achievement and fulfillment in becoming—together—more and more like the One who has led the way, Jesus Christ, Son of Man and Son of God.

So your given talents are important not only to you but to the church also. The gifts of God to the church involve all that is necessary to its life and growth: spiritual insight as well as creative administration, persuasive influence for good as well as discerning challenge to evil.

There are several lists of spiritual gifts in the New Testament. Romans 12 describes prophecy (preaching, inspired utterance), serving others (ministering), teaching (instructing in faith and life), exhorting (encouraging others in faith), contributing to the needs of others (giving aid or sharing with others), leading (administrating, governing with authority), showing mercy (giving sympathy, offering comfort).

First Corinthians 12 adds to the list in a way which focuses on to whom the gifts are given (everyone) and why the gifts are needed (for the good of all).

"The Spirit's presence is shown in some way in each person for the good of all. The Spirit gives one person a message full of wisdom, while to another person the same Spirit gives a message full of knowledge. One and the same Spirit gives faith to one person, while to another person he gives the power to heal. The Spirit gives one person the power to work miracles; to another, the gift of speaking God's message; and to yet another, the ability to tell the difference between gifts that come from the Spirit and those that do not. To one person he gives the ability to speak in strange tongues, and to another he gives the ability to explain what is said. But it is one and the same Spirit who does all this; as he wishes, he gives a different gift to each person" (1 Corinthians 12:7-11, GNB).

For further study—Which gifts listed above are present in your congregation? Of the gifts which seem not to be present, are they: _____ available in nearby congregations, _____ perhaps present but not uncovered, _____ present but not encouraged?

Each one of us is given talents and gifts so that in our lives we can demonstrate the serving love of God to one another and to the world. This is pointed out most effectively by Jesus in the familiar miracle of the feeding of the 5,000 beside the sea of Galilee. It is the most widely known and documented of Jesus' miracles, recorded in each of the Gospels.

As John describes the event (John 6) three distinct messages emerge. In the final one (John 6:35-65), Jesus links Himself to the bread which He multiplied and gave to the hungering crowd. "I am the bread of life," Jesus answers His critics who ask Him to prove He is doing the work of God. "He who comes to me will never be hungry; he who believes in me will never be thirsty. But you, as I said, do not believe although you have seen. (NEB).

The second message is the miracle itself, pointing to the creative dominion God continues to exercise in His world. The boy's five small barley loaves and two little fish are broken to feed the multitude. Perhaps the lad had been sent to sell what he could to the crowd? In any event these meager rations became a hearty meal for 5,000 men and their families. The message? To the crowd it was demonstrated that God meets their needs. Before their eyes the psalmist's faith had been affirmed, "I have been young, and now am old; yet I have not seen the righteous forsaken or his children begging bread" (Psalm 37:25, RSV).

But the initial message was a private lesson to the disciples themselves: a small resource among the congregation of God's people can be multiplied in the unity of their faith.

From the beginning Jesus involves them all in the

situation. He asks Philip what he would do to feed the crowd, and Philip can only admit it is impossible. Andrew finds the boy with his loaves and fishes and although his faith sees a possibility, his incredulity says, "But what are they among so many?"

Then Jesus, "taking the five loaves and the two fish he looked up to heaven, and blessed and broke them, and gave them to the disciples to set before the crowd" (Luke 9:16, RSV).

Working together the disciples shared an experience of ministering to the world with a gift of God. And the church of Christ ever since has ministered the bread of life to a multitude hungering for His reality.

> How has your congregation multiplied the bread of life in your community? In the world beyond? Which seems most appropriate in your experience: _____ all of us, _____ a few of us in the congregation have been involved.

The church struggles with itself today, perhaps because we have held back our gifts. And perhaps like Ananias and Sapphira (Acts 5:1-11) we are dying in the process. We offer only so much of ourselves, unwilling to risk all on Christ and His people.

We see the church as a trap. "If I give my all, I'll have no time for myself." But in reality, what time do we have that has not been given? If we see time as money, we may object to spending what we are without visible profit to us.

But if time is life, then it is spent not in gaining profit but in achieving the character of Christ. In giving life and time to Christ and His church, we gain the meaning of our own lives. For without meaning, life is empty and time is a faceless clock.

"But my life will be used up on silly committees trying to decide on the paint for the church kitchen, or making pies for the annual eat-'til-you're-bowlegged fellowship dinner."

Not if you demand to be used appropriately. If your congregation is so superficial in using the power of God's gifts, then it needs desperately the challenge of your total commitment.

The commitment of your life in full places responsibility upon the body of Christ to use you wisely. Because two are now demanding an adequate response from the church—you yourself, and Christ, the Head of His body.

The superficial church ignores its members' gifts. The cannibal church devours its members to keep itself going. But the living church multiplies the gifts it is given and blesses the lives that are offered.

> Take a survey: How do you feel about full commitment to Christ? Do you feel differently in giving full commitment to the church as to Christ? If so, why?

What then can you do for the church? Submit yourself and your gifts to the people of God. Give of your life, as Christ gave of His. There is no more expected of each of us—and no less.

This isn't an arduous sentence passed upon us by a vindictive judge. God is *love* and *light* and *life*. And as Jesus pointed out, His harness is easy. In fact, the giving of our lives to Christ and His church doesn't mean a heavier load for us to live under. The opposite is true instead. The paradox of submitting our gifts to Christ means a lightening of our lonely, individual striving.

"Come to me," Jesus invites, "all of you who are tired from carrying heavy loads, and I will give you rest. Take my yoke and put it on you, and learn from me, because I am gentle and humble in spirit; and you will find rest. For the yoke I will give you is easy, and the load I will put on you is light" (Matthew 11:28-30, GNB).

The discovery here is the quality of the demand Jesus imposes on our lives. From the world we have learned to expect a harsh reaction to the "weakness of meekness." Instead Jesus and His people impose love, kindness, gentleness, and sharing of burdens. He is gentle and humble in spirit, and that is how He treats our submission to His lordship because His purpose is to make us strong together, "Bear ye one another's burdens, and so fulfil the law of Christ" (Galatians 6:2, KJV).

Humility in serving others with all our gifts opens up our lives to the strength His Spirit can bring. And it is this service—together—which is the meaning of the church, the mysterious meaning which the world sees but can hardly understand.

As Paul tells the Ephesian Christians, "To me, who am less than the least of all God's people, he has granted of his grace the privilege of proclaiming to the Gentiles the good news of the unfathomable riches of Christ, and of bringing to light how this hidden purpose was to be put into effect. It was hidden for long ages in God the creator of the universe, in order that now, through the church, the wisdom of God in all its varied forms might be made known . . ." (Ephesians 3:8-10, NEB).

In giving our time to Christ's life, we will be given the sure freedom to rest and reflect and gain perspective on our lives.

Because we can be sure that Christ will not ask of us the incessant activity of the world, His pace is at peace with Himself. It has been the experience of Christians throughout history that haste and busyness must give way to calm, deliberate, Spirit-led action—if we are to keep pace with God. As poet William Henry Davies questioned:

"What is this life, if full of care,

We have no time to stand and stare?"

Time is life. And in Christ there is an eternity for both. So the lifestyle we are developing together will develop at God's speed. As we commit all that we are to Christ and His church, we can trust that our lives will be fulfilled—gently and lovingly—and for the good of all.

For Christ's yoke is easy and His burden is light.

Transition

From—What you can do for the church

What talents have you discovered and submitted to the church for the congregation's use and benefit? Which gifts are to become part of the congregation's service in the community? Check over your list of major interest-abilities and place them in one or the other of the above categories.

Compare your list with the biblical prototypes in 1 Corinthians 12 and Romans 12. Note particularly the community benefits listed in Romans 12, the basic beginnings of expressing the love of God to neighbors—and even enemies!

Attempt to pin down any restraints you feel at giving your talents to the church. Are you afraid you won't be able to judge when to say "no"? What steps must you take to fully give of yourself yet retain the obligation to follow the inner promptings of the Spirit of God?

To—Part III, Chapter 8, Earning and wages

Part III brings us to the economic resources for our lives: how we earn, what we spend our money on, the rationale for savings plans in a Christian lifestyle, and the vitality of giving of our resources—as individuals and as a church.

Earning a living involves the major investment of our time. It has its problems financially, but also psychologically and spiritually. Working should be a pleasure if we exercise our gifts as God would have us do.

But who or what is to determine the level of income we receive? Christian employers can demonstrate the freeing jubilee of the Lord in the prices they set and the wages they pay. Further, Christian employers can include their employees in decision-making as well as in providing for "unemployables."

In Chapter 8 earning emerges as the potential for satisfactory freedom, the freedom to meet other's needs as well as our own. See 2 Thessalonians 3:6-13; Leviticus 25:8-55; Luke 4:14-22.

Part III, Chapter 8—Earning and wages

A. Choosing a suitable job.
    1. Many work only for money.
    2. Working is wholesome.
        a. Idleness is wrong (2 Thessalonians 3:10-12).
        b. Working brings satisfaction (2 Thessalonians 3:7-9).
        c. Buddhist example of work satisfaction.

B. Standards for wages and income.
    1. Christian employee attitudes illustrated.
    2. Congregation can give counsel.
    3. Professional fee-setting.
        a. Can fees be too low?
        b. Alternative for low-income clients.

C. Jubilee employment.
    1. A congregation finds jobs.
    2. Employer attempts jubilee.
        a. By profit sharing.
        b. By stock options.
        c. By employee/management committee.
        d. By hiring "unemployables" (Luke 4:16-21).

Part III
The Elements of Power:
Personal Resources in Mission

8
Earning and wages

> ... it has often occurred to me that with the many Mennonite Brethren in land development, construction, real estate, and generally in all aspects of the building trades, if all of them resolved to work hard at making housing available at the most reasonable price possible, it would surely make a difference within the whole country.
>
> It is a scandal that in a nation with the amount of land that we have and with the lumber resources available to us, land and housing should cost what it does. The only reason one can finally give to it is that far too many people have been in the housing and real estate industry only for the unusual profits they could make. They have exploited their neighbors.
>
> —Harold Jantz in *Mennonite Brethren Herald*

Most of us don't have a choice whether to work or not. We want to eat, buy some clothes, invest in a car, and the most acceptable process to achieve these ends is to find gainful employment.

And for most of us the choice of jobs is fairly narrow— or so we think. We take on a job that opens up. Then we take on the time payments for a car. And forever after we're locked into the cycle of "too much month at the end of our money."

We become slaves to our wants. With the pressure of bills, we commit ourselves to earning any kind of money in order to buy ourselves free. But because we have started out on the downhill side, we can't get ahead.

So we take on a moonlighting job. But the faster the money comes in, the faster it goes out, and "the hurrieder we go, the behinder we get."

We become victims of the ages-old ploy of the devil to enslave us to our own hungers. And the freedom God wants for us is always just beyond our fingertips—

"Lord, don't call me, 'cause I can't go.
I sold my soul to the company store."

Yes, it is right to work. And work hard. As the Apostle Paul told the Thessalonians sitting around waiting for Christ to come back and make them princes in His kingdom:

" 'If a man will not work, he shall not eat.'

"We hear that some among you are idle," Paul continues. "They are not busy; they are busybodies. In the name of the Lord Jesus Christ, we command and urge such people to settle down and earn the bread they eat" (2 Thessalonians 3:10-12, NIV—see also 1 Thessalonians 4:9-12).

Here Paul is dealing with another common form of slavery: dependency. Persons can become psychologically disabled by expecting others to provide for their needs when they are physically able to work.

Paul knew something that we tend to forget—work is rewarding in more ways than the financial. That is, if we set ourselves to build a wholesome life around our God-given interest-abilities in doing what God wants us to do. Through our work we can achieve that unique satisfaction which comes only in serving others.

That means setting goals for our work-lives instead of becoming slaves to a job for the sake of what it can earn.

What goals? They can be as simple as to set a good example. In the same letter, Paul tells the Christians at Thessalonica, "For you yourselves know how you ought to follow our example. We were not idle when we were with you, nor did we eat anyone's food without paying for it. On the contrary, we worked night and day, laboring and toiling so that we would not be a burden to any of you. We did this, not because we do not have the right to such help, but in order to make ourselves a model for you to follow" (2 Thessalonians 3:7-9, NIV).

What could be some other goals for working? What goals would you like to achieve from your present job?

Dr. E. F. Schumacher, Rhodes scholar and British economist, spent a number of exploratory visits in Burma, India, and other developing countries. He saw a notable difference in Buddhist countries in the approach of the working people to their jobs.

"There is universal agreement that a fundamental source of wealth is human labor," Schumacher writes in his essay, *Thinking Differently: Buddhist Economics.*° "Now, the modern economist has been brought up to consider 'labor' or work as little more than a necessary evil. . . . From the point of view of the workman, it is a 'disutility'; to work is to make a sacrifice of one's leisure and comfort, and wages are a kind of compensation for the sacrifice. . . .

"The Buddhist point of view takes the function of work to be at least threefold: to give a man a chance to

---

°Included in *Economic Power Failure: The Current American Crisis*, edited by Summer M. Rosen, New York: McGraw-Hill Book Company, 1975.

utilize and develop his faculties; to enable him to overcome his ego-centeredness by joining with other people
in a common task; and to bring forth the goods and
services needed for a becoming existence. To organize
work in such a manner that it becomes meaningless, bor-
ing, stultifying, or nerve-racking for the worker would be
little short of criminal; it would indicate a greater
concern with goods than with people. . . . Equally, to
strive for leisure as an alternative to work would be
considered a complete misunderstanding of one of the
basic truths of human existence, namely that work and
leisure are complementary parts of the same living
process and cannot be separated without destroying the
joy of work and the bliss of leisure."

The worker deserves his wages—but what kind of
wages? How much should the laborer demand? What
fees should the doctor or consultant set? What level of income should we expect from our business?

Harry worked as a cabinetmaker for a sash and door
company. He believed in rendering a good day's work for
his wages, which he negotiated for himself with the
owner. "Unions use coercion," Harry used to say, and
would have nothing to do with organized labor. He tried
to live as a servant of Jesus Christ, his wages and the way
he negotiated them was as much a part of his walk with
Christ as studying for the adult Bible class he taught
every Sunday.

But his brother Bert would like to see the workers
organized in some way at the shop where he works. They
make a line of concrete blocks for buildings and farm
silos. It's a highly competitive business and the wages are
consistently low.

"The boss doesn't suffer though," complains Bert.

"He's making a good profit, and he pays himself a big salary. I don't care that he puts a lot of time and money into the Lord's work—that time and money come out of his employees' labor."

Harry reproves Bert for his attitude. "You should be grateful for a Christian boss. He gives you steady work the year around and pays you as good—maybe better than you'd get from his competitors. It's because he's honest and a good businessman that he gets the contracts to keep you all busy. And he's got a big investment in the factory."

Bert argues back, "But why doesn't he give some of us the privilege of serving the Lord like he does? I would like to get a couple weeks off—with pay—to help in Mennonite Disaster Service, for instance. But he can't afford that, he says.

"He'll give us time off to do it on our own—but without pay I can't afford to take off time even to be sick."

Should Bert take his wage problem to his congregation? It should be possible for any member to ask for counsel from the church, even on such a threatening subject as personal income. And Bert's boss should be able to find encouragement for his wage scale—and his own salary—in the context of fellowship. Insofar as these matters are taboo among us indicates how sensitive we are to the opinions of others on financial matters.

It will take more than one Sunday evening panel to develop the openness for congregational participation in wage discussions. The risks involved call for a wisely gentle approach, with the first step restricted to the establishing of some general guidelines. Then your group should test these guidelines on a series of hypothetical examples—which may or may not be close to local reality.

But in spite of the risks, the loving support of the people of God provides the most appropriate setting for understanding both sides, because there are two sides in every wage discussion—and both need to be exposed to the Spirit of God through the people of God.

> What might be the factors which fix your wages at their present level? What might cause them to increase? To decrease? How might your congregation advise you?

A Mennonite doctor in semiretirement serves a clientele who can neither afford medical insurance nor the higher fees his younger colleagues charge. In doing so, his reputation has suffered amongst more well-to-do patients.

A younger doctor, Clair Weaver of Norlanco Clinic in Lancaster County, Pennsylvania, acknowledges that this process can happen. He and his associates are committed to serving Jesus Christ with their medical skills. "If a doctor sets his fees too low, people may doubt his ability. Although we charge a relatively low fee for our area, there are still some people who are unable to pay their bills. So we have built in a device which allows anyone on a low income to pay what he can—and we accept that as payment in full."

Dr. Weaver and his associates arrange their schedules to permit each one to take time off for study or service after a number of months' work. He himself has served in Haiti under Medical Group Missions, an agency providing volunteer medical services to needy areas in the name of Christ. Others have taken specialized training in order to keep up with developments in their specialty.

These young medical men are sharing in a fellowship of service, as are other similar groups, yet not as some congregations who practice a fellowship of earning such as Reba Place Fellowship in Evanston, Illinois. This congregation has long lived out the principle of "all things in common," at least insofar as pooling the income of all the wage earners and dividing to each according to his need.

The Bethesda Mennonite Church in St. Louis' Ward 19 has worked in another way—almost as a fellowship of employment. This congregation and its leaders have been stimulators and creative resources within an economically depressed area. Through their work with other Christian and community leaders, a shoe company moved into the community, providing over 400 jobs for local residents. Macler Shepard, chairman of Bethseda's church council, finds his service to Christ and His church as the placement officer for Jeff-Vander-Lou, as the community organization is called. It not only serves to place local residents in shoe company jobs, but also in scores of other businesses throughout the area.

Jubilee is an unusual facet of redemption which deals with economics. It comes from the word of the Lord to Moses on Mount Sinai: "And you shall hallow the fiftieth year, and proclaim liberty throughout the land to all its inhabitants; it shall be a jubilee for you, when each of you shall return to his property" (Leviticus 25:10, RSV).

Jubilee recognizes the inequities which accumulated wealth can impose upon a society. Through disaster or other circumstance a family can lose its homestead and lose its potential for economic survival. Always the loss is to another, who through favorable circumstance is able to buy his neighbor's potential and add it to his own. The results have tended to echo throughout succeeding generations as wealth or poverty is passed on to children's children in an inheritance of advantage or disadvantage, power or powerlessness, capital or the lack of it.

But to protect His people from the injustices of "blind fate," God commanded the children of Israel to observe the jubilee: allowing the original holder's family to repossess their land. In this act, potential for survival was renewed. And potential meant freedom, even for the indentured servant: "And if your brother becomes poor beside you, and sells himself to you, you shall not make him serve as a slave: he shall be with you as a hired servant and as a sojourner. He shall serve with you until the year of jubilee; then he shall go out from you, he and his children with him, and go back to his own family, and return to the possession of his fathers" (Leviticus 25:39-41, RSV).

What can jubilee mean in the tangled webs of advantage and power and accumulated wealth today? The Bethesda congregation is working at restoring potential to the disadvantaged in St. Louis. The work of Mennonite Disaster Service in rebuilding the shattered hopes of earthquake victims in Guatemala is another example.

> Take a survey: What situations in North America call for jubilee? If land cannot be returned to its original owners, how can justice be achieved? Can jubilee be satisfied by money payments? Welfare? What are the jubilee needs in your congregation? What might your people have to restore in your community?

Wilmer Thomson is a successful businessman who has long attempted to be fully Christlike in his relations with his employees and his customers alike. He has established a policy of warranted quality in the products his company produces. The policy is sustained in a market economy which is at times fiercely competitive.

He also attempts jubilee in four distinct ways. The first, profit sharing, recognizes that the success of the company in maintaining its share-of-market depends upon the willing participation of employees not only in production rates but also in product quality.

While profit-sharing has become a practice of a number of businesses, Wilmer's Christian convictions have led him to go futher by offering shares of company stock as an alternative to cash bonuses. Not many have opted for the shares, since it involves some future risk in place of immediate dollars. But some employees are accumulating responsible levels of ownership, and the option continues for all others.

Wilmer goes still further in a regular schedule of "policy and direction-planning" meetings which also involve employees on an equal footing with management. He has been accused of doing so as a means of frustrating union attempts to organize his shop. But as he insists, "I will accept any organization our employees choose as long as it will allow the employees to act for their own good on our policy and direction-planning team." So far no union local has been willing to adapt its national directives to include such an innovation. And the employees have rejected any union efforts to limit this activity.

"But I expect one day one of the unions will accept this as the advantage it is for them," Wilmer asserts, "and when it does we will be happy to work with them on the team."

The fourth step of jubilee action Wilmer's company takes is to hire "unemployables"—those misfits to any economic system who have limited abilities in doing the kind of work our system demands. These persons may have limited training, little schooling, or disabling physical or mental handicaps. One may be a widowed mother, who has been out of the job market for so long that she needs sympathetic patience from an employer until she regains confidence and assurance.

"The first unemployable I hired," Wilmer recalls, "had been in and out of a number of unskilled jobs. He was none too bright, and couldn't seem to remember instructions. He was unreliable—if he needed to clean out his chicken pen he'd stay home and do it.

"He said he was too old to learn new tricks—yet he wanted to have the money a job would provide. He complained continually about the companies who had fired him before, I think it was his way of anticipating failure again. But he also blamed other employees for the mistakes he made and that got him into increasing troubles with his co-workers.

"I finally had to let him go. We weren't able to cope with his disruptive behavior. But we learned by the experience. The Christian workers in the shop were embarrassed at their failure too, so we tried together to figure out why we hadn't been able to help him.

"So our policy and planning team set up a new-employees group to help any new worker with the adjustments necessary to make it in the shop. Since then we've hired a number of people who have had trouble finding and holding a job. A couple of them have needed professional counsel and we've paid for that too."

These "unemployables" are all still working at

Wilmer's shop. It would be nice to say they had rewarded his jubilee efforts by becoming top producers. But that isn't true. Only one holds promise of being a better-than-average producer as far as company output is concerned.

Yet that isn't the point. Wilmer and the employees team have taken seriously their privilege of helping others. And that has proven to be a satisfying possibility for them in a work of jubilee.

"So [Jesus] . . . came to Nazareth, where he had been brought up, and went to synagogue on the Sabbath day as he regularly did. He stood up to read the lesson and was handed the scroll of the prophet Isaiah. He opened the scroll and found the passage which says,

'The Spirit of the Lord is upon me because he has anointed me; he has sent me to announce good news to the poor,

to proclaim release for prisoners and recovery of sight for the blind;

to let the broken victims go free,

to proclaim the year of the Lord's favour (jubilee)'. . . .

"Today," he said "in your very hearing this text has come true" (Luke 4:16-21, NEB).

Transition
From—Earning and wages

The amount that you earn is a function of your vocation. How satisfying are the *serving* functions of your job? What other elements of your job are as important to you as wages? (Consider time with your family and friends, location, church fellowship, opportunity to serve others, etc.) What elements of your work other than wages tend to make it less than satisfactory? (Consider product, location, time away from friends and family, worker environment and relationships, etc.) What might you do to increase your satisfactions and decrease your problems in your work?

Evaluate your talent-interests in terms of your present work and jubilee. Are you using your gift-abilities fully? If not, what goals must be set in order to bring your talents and work-life together and bring you into closer fellowship in your congregation? Ask for discussion of this in your class or midweek meeting.

To—Chapter 9, Spending your income

Anybody can spend money, but not everyone can control their impulses to buy. North Americans live in a society where consumption is a virtue and advertising the encouraging force. The problems of consumption can induce tension in home, church, and community, so the Christian needs to achieve control in spending.

Jesus does not encourage tightfisted parsimony any more than affluent self-indulgence. So spending is a skill to be developed in a lifestyle for mission. Skills include analysis of spending, first to establish where the money goes. Then with guidelines, the group can work at developing personal spending patterns "to the glory of God."

In Chapter 9 controlled spending becomes a skill to achieve freedom from a consumer lifestyle. See John 2:1-11; Luke 16:19-31; Luke 12:13-34.

Chapter 9—Spending your income

A. Christian spending patterns.
     1. Contrast in two weddings.
     2. A place for openhanded spending.
     3. Two ditches on either side.
          a. Self-gratifying overindulgence (Luke 16:19-31).
          b. Parsimonious stinginess (Luke 12:13-34).

B. Spending skills.
     1. Avoid pressured buying.

2. Minimize energy consumption.
3. Analyze spending habits.
   a. Keep notebook of expenditures.
   b. Resource: MMA guide.
   c. Key to economizing: "as unto the Lord."

9
Spending your income

One of the especially dangerous things about the love of money is its ability to mask itself as something entirely different from its true character. It may pose as a very commendable diligence in caring for financial resources and opportunities. It may present itself to the head of a household as fulfilling the scriptural injunction to "provide for his own." It may assert itself under the guise of maintaining integrity in handling and meeting financial obligations (notwithstanding its determining influence in the decisions to incur the obligations in the first place). It may even represent itself as "Christian stewardship." Its masquerades are virtually unlimited, and often so convincing that those involved are themselves quite deceived.
—John M. Snyder in *Sword and Trumpet*

A tale of two weddings: Naomi Webber's and Carolyn Martin's. Naomi and Carolyn are second cousins and see each other occasionally at the Martin family reunion. The girls are the same age and both were married in September to boys they met at school.

Both girls come from well-to-do families. Carolyn's father is an astute farmer, Naomi's father owns several tracts of real estate on the developing edges of the city which swallowed up his childhood home in the boom after World War II.

There the similarity begins to fade. Carolyn and Bruce

were married during the morning service at her church. The congregation—swollen by the many guests which came to join in the happy occasion—stood as the couple exchanged their vows. Following the sermon, the congregation and the guests moved downstairs for a meal. Along one wall tables had been set up to receive the wedding gifts which friends brought to give the young couple a start.

Naomi and Greg received a number of helpful gifts too—but their wedding took place on a Saturday, and only invited guests attended. The bride looked especially beautiful in the gown which she had made herself. Her bridesmaids were also lovely in their gowns and matching shoes which—as one girl pointed out wistfully—cost her most of a week's wages.

The reception afterward wasn't a big affair, but since it was handled by caterers, it did cost Naomi's father more money than the home-cooked meal Carolyn's family and friends provided.

The cost? There is no doubt that Carolyn's wedding cost less than Naomi's. But since both were comparatively modest and both families well-to-do, neither family was seriously inconvenienced.

Yet a year later, other significant differences are beginning to show up. Both families had invested a goodly amount of money and time in the weddings. But *how* they spent themselves and their money is gathering momentum.

Carolyn and Bruce chose to set their wedding within a recommitment to Jesus Christ and His church. It meant deemphasizing their own moment of glory. "We expect it will be difficult enough for us to keep up a good attitude toward the church," Carolyn explains. "So many of our friends are off-again, on-again about church and what it can ask of us.

"That's why we felt we should be married in the midst of the congregation. To help us think of our marriage in terms of the people of God."

What about Naomi and Greg? No, their marriage hasn't fallen apart. And they haven't turned their backs on God and the church. But the memory of their wedding tends to reinforce an indifference toward the church and its influence on their lives.

This major investment of feelings and time and finances seems to have isolated them further in a growing independence from the community of God. Where did Naomi and her parents get their ideas for the wedding ceremony? From the wedding notices in their paper. From *Woman's Day* magazine. And from weddings of friends and acquaintances.

When it comes to spending our money and our time, we are fair game for the advertisers and persuaders. Christians aren't immune from the blandishments of those who have a lifestyle to sell.

"Marriage is big business," *Bride's Magazine* tells prospective advertisers. At the top of a full page promotion in *Advertising Age*, the headline declares, "*When she says 'I do,' she means 'I'll buy.'* "

The ad for *Bride's Magazine* goes on, "She'll be buying $8 billion worth of goods and services during a concentrated one year period from engagement to wedding to setting up home." The ad then lists some of the many products newlyweds require, before and after the ceremony: clothing, furniture, cookware, honeymoon travel, dishes and cutlery (the ad calls it "china and silverware" to give it some class), appliances, insurance, credit services, automobiles, linens, food and health aids, and on and on.

The ad shows a bride with a faraway look in her eye and a dream floating above her head—not of her husband, but of a crowd of gadgets and furnishings and beauty aids. And a cover of the magazine claims in large print, "Your Complete Wedding Planner."

So it is little wonder that Naomi and Greg remember their wedding as a grand event. Because that's what it was. But Carolyn and Bruce chose more wisely, resisting the Madison Avenue touch so their memories could achieve some meaning.

How much should a wedding cost? _____ more than a month's wages, _____less than a month's wages, _____as little as possible. Who should decide? Should the congregation set guidelines? Why?

Life needs its grand events. When Jesus turned water into wine for the wedding party at Cana, He also turned an imminent embarrassment into a memorable celebration. There are times when joyous openhanded spending is right. And a family festival such as a wedding is just such a time. At Cana, a village in Galilee, the wedding guests included Mary the mother of Jesus. He and the disciples were invited also (see John 2:1-11).

It could be that the happy couple were related to Mary and Jesus. Because when the wine ran out, Mary told her Son about it. It's hard to tell from the little scrap of conversation the Bible records just what Mary and Jesus talked about. It appears that Jesus wanted to avoid a dramatic display of heaven's power such as His later miracles which so focused the attention of the people on His ministry.

But Jesus also agrees with His mother that something must be done to avoid the embarrassing failure of the party. Perhaps' He felt some responsibility for the extra guests and the added gaiety—in any event the wine was gone, and the celebration would soon wind down. So Jesus prepared this quiet miracle (which only John's Gospel recalls). When the servants fill the water-jars with water and take some to the master of ceremonies, the man is surprised. Instead of following good wine with inferior, this was of excellent quality, better than the first wine.

And instead of disheartening shortage at their wedding feast, the friends of Jesus enjoyed abundant blessing.

There is a ditch on either side of the spending way—easy to fall into, hard to escape. On the right is self-gratifying overindulgence. On the left is parsimonious stinginess.

Some people are closefisted with their money, "as tight as the bark on a tree," the saying goes. For them, no amount of money is enough. And strangely, their problem is similar to those who overindulge; both exhibit a powerful selfishness.

In the Gospel according to Luke, Jesus tells two parables of wealthy men, one who continually overindulges himself; and one who promises himself a lavish time when he finally has enough. The rich man who feasts sumptuously every day has ignored the poor man who begs every day for table scraps from the rich man's table. When the two men die, the rich man finds himself in Hades while Lazarus is carried by angels to Abraham's bosom.

In remorse at his self-indulgent lifestyle, the rich man

cries to Abraham to send Lazarus to warn his brothers not to make the same mistake. But as Jesus points out, even if someone were to return from the dead, those whose lives are self-indulged would ignore his warning (Luke 16:19-31).

In the other parable Jesus tells of the rich man whose land gave him bumper crops, so much so that his storage buildings weren't big enough. Now, as Jesus said, "A man's life does not consist in the abundance of his possessions" (Luke 12:15, RSV). But for this man, abundance was not enough.

So he expands. He tears down his buildings and builds larger ones. That is his lifestyle: accumulate, sock it away, amass more—then he can say to his soul, "Soul, you have ample goods laid up for many years; take your ease, eat, drink, be merry" (Luke 12:19, RSV).

But that time never arrives for him. God steps in first and says, "Fool! This night your soul is required of you; and the things you have prepared, whose will they be?" (Luke 12:20, RSV).

The selfishness of hoarding is as deadly for us as overindulgence. In either case our eyes are centered on ourselves rather than on God and His way of living. "So is he," Jesus concludes the parable, "who lays up treasure for himself, and is not rich toward God" (Luke 12:21, RSV).

> How much wealth does it take to produce covetousness? How much poverty? Are there levels of poverty which are satisfying? Are there levels which are unhealthy?

The skill in spending is, like the writer of Proverbs, to "Trust in the Lord with all your heart, and do not rely on your own insight. In all your ways acknowledge him, and he will make straight your paths" (Proverbs 3:5, 6, RSV. See also Luke 12:22-34).

That's a lot different from becoming a consumer just to keep the consumer society going. If consuming is our end then we are processors of goods, not people.

But we live in a consumer society. Our daily newspapers are full of beguiling advertisements. Television programs leapfrog over 30-second commercial injections. Radio stations mark success by the customers they bring to the businesses who advertise between the newscasts and the disc jockeys.

In this climate of urged consumption, freedom to live Christ's way means controlled spending, spending-with-a-purpose.

Norma has struggled to control her spending. When energy began its escalation several years ago, she determined to stay ahead of its burden if she could.

As she analyzed the problem, she became increasingly aware of the number of energy-consuming gadgets people were being talked into. So her first efforts were to explore what she could do without.

Norma has resisted electric can-openers and toothbrushes and dishwashers. But her biggest discovery came as she analyzed the power used by her laundry equipment. She decided to dry her clothes on the line. "I get the exercise and fresh air, and the laundry smells so much fresher," she says as she explains why she sold her dryer.

Then came another discovery. When she figured out the hot water used in her automatic washer, and compared its power consumption with a wringer machine, she made another deal. She sold her energy expensive automatic washer and bought an inexpensive wringer type.

"Then I got a surprise! I expected it would take me more time and labor. Not so! I'm actually freer now than I was with my so-called labor-saving devices. I finish my laundry in less time overall and I'm happier with the results—and our electric bills are less."

The most important step in controlling expenditures is analyzing your spending habits. Unfortunately it is easier said than done. Like dieting, we can see its value. But getting a workable program going seems like too much work.

Yet analyzing spending is the single most helpful device for quickly putting yourself in control of your finances. While most of us struggle along from paycheck to paycheck wondering where it all goes—and looking for moonlighting jobs to bail us out—others who have learned to control spending know that is the answer.

Few of us have any power over the wages we get, or the inflation which shrinks our buying power. But we can spend less than Madison Avenue wants us to.

It isn't hard to analyze spending. Start with a couple of pocket notebooks. As you fill your shopping cart, list every item and its cost. Whenever you stop at a store, write down what you buy.

Yes, you'll forget, and feel as if you've messed things up. But hang in there, the times you forget will be fewer as you get into the swing of it. And, like dieting, the results will be rewarding if you keep at it.

Step two is to group your purchases into some logical categories. There are budgeting plans you can buy from various sources which have the categories listed. My wife wrote for the program put out by Cornell University, Ithaca, New York. (Bulletin 86, $1.00). They suggest 50 items under nine basic groupings.

Mennonite Mutual Aid has an eight-page booklet, *A Christian's Spending Guide*, with an excellent outline of 19 items under two groupings:

1. Fixed expenditures which come regularly each week, month or year: church donations; housing (rent or mortgage); past debt installments; car payments, insurance and license; retirement; health and life insurance; taxes.

2. Variable expenditures which can be controlled: housing (heat, electricity, water, maintenance); credit card debts; transportation (gas, maintenance); retirement/savings; medical/dental; clothing/personal care; recreation; food; allowances.

The booklet includes a spending plan with suggested guidelines on how to establish and check a budget:

1. The traditional figure for church giving is 10 percent.

2. You shouldn't pay more than 2½-3 years' income in buying a house.

3. Past debts should not use more than 20 to 30 percent of a year's income.

4. Transportation should not cost more than 12.5 percent of your income.

5. Try to accumulate from three to six months' income as an emergency fund. Savings could amount to from 5 to 9 percent of your budget.

6. You should have from two to three years' income in life insurance or survivors' protection. You shouldn't pay more than 4 to 5 percent of your income on life insurance.

7. Clothing should not exceed 7.5 percent of your yearly budget.

8. Recreation shouldn't use more than 10 percent of your budget.

As the *Guide* points out, a Christian committed to a life of discipleship and service may need to adjust these guidelines to "do all to the glory of God."

The *Guide* assumes a group process as your congregation explores making money work for discipleship. So four goals are suggested for your group:

"Through this experience we hope to gain:

"a. Greater faithfulness in our use of money.

"b. Greater openness among ourselves about the proper uses of money.

"c. Greater control over the use of money, with less impulsive and compulsive buying and spending.

"d. Greater freedom to use money to express our faith."

From the *Guide*—What pressures do we feel from our society concerning the use of money? What is the Christian attitude toward money and property in contrast to society's attitude? How do we decide how to spend our money? How can you work together in your group to help each other make decisions on the best use of money and property?

In analyzing your spending you can follow the *Guide's* outline, find an outline in the "budgeting" section in your public library, or devise your own. A simple device that works is to buy two school notebooks. Number the pages in the first one. Then begin to list your purchases on separate pages: one for cereals, one for fresh fruit, one for cleaning supplies, etc. Keep one page, perhaps the first or last one, as an index.

Then when you have used your first notebook for a month or two, reorganize your system of pages into the second one and start again. By this time you will have gained much good experience.

What will such an analysis show you? First, it will give you precise information on your spending habits. Second, you will have the information needed to make necessary cuts.

Cornell's program points out that by analyzing expenditures you will be able to tell when and where to shop for better prices *because you already have a record of the prices you have paid.*

It will take time. But you will be able to make decisions which will save you many, many dollars. And you will have the basic information you need for the next most important step in controlling spending: never go shopping without knowing what—and how much of it—you want to buy.

The principle is to cut down on impulse buying. Some shoppers eat before going to the supermarket just to ensure that appetite won't overrule good judgement.

Since we can talk ourselves into anything, it is good to develop the opposite tactic in asking, "Is this something I can do without?"

Affluent consumption is a learned experience. So is living simply, "as unto the Lord." Disciplined living is freedom: freedom to live within the easy partnership of Christ's yoke, freedom from slavery to the consumer style of life.

Transition
From—Spending your income

E. F. Schumacher describes four levels of existence—on the bottom, *misery.* Then *poverty,* where life can be lived with some joy and dignity. The third level is *sufficiency,* with something to spare. Finally is *surfeit,* too much of everything. The bottom and top levels are demeaning to the spirit. What level do you believe the Christian should seek to achieve? Why? Is there a "non-Christian" level?

How does guilt influence your spending patterns? Some persons reject guilt feelings and become insulated against any limitations on spending, even to the point of overspending. Others' guilt creates a negative attitude toward persons who feel free to spend. How do you feel toward others who spend more than you? Why?

To—Chapter 10, Saving for what future?

As the saying goes, "It isn't what you handle, but what you get to keep that counts." Saving for the future depends upon the kind and quality of future you must have. Family and friends are assets for the future, as is the growing relationship in the body of Christ.

Money savings are not the only way to prepare for the future. Gardening, cooperative ownership, credit unions are additional means of saving.

And the major security of the Christian rests in the promises of God to provide for all who will seek first His kingdom's way of living. While this may test the disciple's position in a consumer society, it remains the simplifying core of a trusting lifestyle.

In Chapter 10, planning for a secure future leads to increased awareness of the people of God among whom our trust in Christ may mature, as over against our trust in the systems of the world. See Matthew 6:19-34; 1 John 2:15-17.

Chapter 10—Saving for what future?

A. Christian preparations for the future.
    1. One elderly Christian's attitude.
    2. Problem of independence.
    3. Jesus teaches preparation (Matthew 6:19-34).
    4. Can the future be protected?

B. Mutual care of the people of God vs individualism.
  1. Independence is admired.
  2. Mobility encourages individualism.
  3. Mutual caring and sharing builds strength in community.

C. Savings programs for a focused lifestyle.
  1. Begin with an "anywhere" garden.
  2. Yard sales for cash.
  3. Cooperative ownership.
  4. Credit unions.
  5. Debt reduction.
      a. Start now tightening your belt.
      b. Schedule essential spending.
      c. Divide old debts into payment schedule.
      d. Seek counsel (1 Corinthians 12:26).
  6. Christ's way is better (1 John 1:15-17).

10
Saving for what future?

Behold the fowls of the air: for they sow not, neither do they reap, nor gather into barns; yet your heavenly Father feedeth them. Are ye not much better than they?. . . Consider the lilies of the field, how they grow; they toil not, neither do they spin: yet I say unto you, That even Solomon in all his glory was not arrayed like one of these. . . . Therefore take no thought, saying, What shall we eat? or, What shall we drink? or, Wherewithal shall we be clothed? . . . for your heavenly Father knoweth that ye have need of all these things. But seek ye first the kingdom of God, and his righteousness; and all these things shall be added unto you. Take therefore no thought for the morrow (Matthew 6:26-34, KJV).

Neither anxiety nor work can secure [the Christian's] daily bread, for bread is the gift of the Father. The birds and lilies neither toil nor spin, yet both are fed and clothed and receive their daily portion without being anxious for them. . . . "Man-in-revolt" imagines that there is a relation of cause and effect between work and sustenance, but Jesus explodes that illusion. According to him, bread is not to be valued as the reward for work; he speaks instead of the carefree simplicity of the man who walks with him and accepts everything as it comes from God. . . .

Worldly cares are not a part of our discipleship, but distinct and subordinate concerns. Before we start taking thought for our life, our food and clothing, our work and families, we must seek the righteousness of Christ. This is no more than an ultimate summing up of all that has been said before. Again we have here either a crushing burden, which holds out no hope for the poor and wretched, or else it is the quintessence of the gospel, which brings the promise of freedom and perfect joy. . . . If we follow Jesus and look only to his righteousness, we are in his hands and under the protection of him and his Father. And if we are in communion with the Father, nought can harm us. We shall always be assured that he can feed his children and will not suffer them to hunger. God will help us in the hour of need, and he knows our needs."

—Dietrich Bonhoeffer in *The Cost of Discipleship*

When all her children and grandchildren come to Ivy Moyers' house for Christmas dinner, there isn't room for anybody to fall down, as she puts it. She's pushing 78 now, and may be more independent than ever, although one or other of her daughters will call her on the phone most every day. A son often comes around to check on her, particularly if he has some beef grazing on the land he rents next door.

Come Sunday afternoon, several cars will be parked in her yard as her children stop by to visit her—and each other (cf. Exodus 20:12).

Ivy keeps a few chickens, some Guinea hens, and raises a couple of calves every year to pay for her coal and taxes. The last couple years since coal has gone up, she burns more wood in the heater which occupies a major position in her parlor.

Ivy does more than survive on social security. She *lives*. Her garden is big enough to feed a dozen people. And she digs into her calf money for Christmas gifts for her grandchildren and a few neighbors as well.

Ivy isn't alone. For many years she has trusted Jesus

Christ, and her life shows it. And she has given of her life to others. Now in her old age, the trust of a lifetime continues. In spite of the absence of accumulated wealth, Ivy is rich in the people who love her.

We can see Ivy Moyers' little home from our porch. There are few people today who would care to live as simply as Ivy does. Or without the security of a bank account or retirement trust to cushion the indignities of advancing age. But few are as secure as she in the abiding care of the kingdom of God.

> Take a survey: How many of your friends or persons in your group live close to any members of their families or near relatives? What happens to orphans, widows, single people in your community? In your congregation?

In our culture, independence is admired. But Ivy is independent of people's pity, not of people. Her days have never been so busy that she doesn't welcome visitors, or baby-sit for a neighbor, or help round up a straying steer.

"But where would she be without social security?" Some people will always challenge the simple lifestyle of an Ivy Moyers, if only to justify the need for a more elaborate manner of living for themselves.

Yet if we had no social security system, Ivy would probably fare as well or better—comparatively—as she does now. We tend to forget that in the present shape of our economic system, Ivy pays a higher percentage of her income in sales and excise taxes than ever before. We have built a complex society—and it can be demonstrated that sales and excise taxes impose a heavier burden proportionately on those who must spend all their income than those who have some left over for savings. So that in a simpler economy, while Ivy may have had to sell eggs to meet her taxes, the eggs might have been more than enough to pay the simpler tariffs.

"Ah, but she had land!" True, but even in this era of skyrocketing land values, her humble homestead—like hundreds of thousands similar to it in less prestigious neighborhoods of country or city—would not cost as much as many people spend on recreational vehicles or boats.

> List the essential items you buy which are subject to sales or excise taxes. Consider how much these taxes have increased as product prices have increased. What might be the effect on persons with low fixed incomes?

So in her simple surroundings Ivy Moyers is more independent of the demands of society than most of us. Like the birds or wildflowers Jesus spoke about, she has not wasted her years in anxiety for tomorrow.

Of course, she gathers her garden produce and stores it away for the winter. Jesus could have talked about the squirrels and bees whose industrious storing make it possible to survive the long dormant months.

But Jesus knew that the human problem isn't putting by enough for tomorrow. We go beyond simple preparation for tomorrow to elaborate accumulation. And we grow to depend more upon our worldly savings than upon our heavenly Father's care.

"Do not lay up for yourselves treasures on earth," Jesus instructed His disciples, "where moth and rust consume and where thieves break in and steal, but lay up for yourselves treasures in heaven, where neither moth nor rust consumes and where thieves do not break in and steal. For where your treasure is, there will your heart be also" (Matthew 6:19-21, RSV).

How much is enough? For many people government programs will not provide adequate incomes for retirement. Some company pensions add substantial benefits. And individual retirement accounts make it possible now for anyone to save for those so-called "golden years" of enforced inactivity—if the money becomes available to save.

Some people will not reach retirement. The actuarial possibilities for an interrupted future are legion—and so are the ways people have devised to hedge against these uncertainties: life insurance, health coverage, travel and accident protection, liability coverage, fire and theft, burial aid, income insurance, among many others.

For the Christian it becomes a question of the individualism of these multiplied protection plans. It is certain that the believer who attempts to live simply in faith will feel some tension with the advertising which pushes him to protect against all the circumstances of the future, *by himself.*

In our society the ability of the individual to make it on his own is highly admired. The corollary is his ability to look after himself and his family in any form of emergency. This tends to isolate a person further from neighbors. Individualism has become the norm rather than community sharing. Efforts at mutual caring and sharing have tended to be weakened further through our high mobility in changing jobs and moving to new neighborhoods.

But the kingdom of God points to another reality in which individualism is neither a strength nor an advantage. Within a caring and sharing community the shocks of unexpected circumstance can be absorbed with healing love.

Furthermore, mutual aid builds strength in community. As we help one another, we put muscles on the bones of commitment. We learn to care as we care. We learn love as we reach out to those who need our love.

Jesus commanded His disciples to love one another for this very reason. Although on the surface it may seem selfish for Christians to love one another ("shouldn't they love the stranger first?" the skeptic asks.), it is a matter of practical discipline. As we love and build each other up in the body of Christ we are building our ability to love the world *in the way it needs our love*. No one can simply strike out on his own to love as Jesus loved. It is a learned discipline, grown in the fellowship of mutual aid and burden bearing.

Together in the body of Christ we are greater than the sum of our individual lives. Mennonite Mutual Aid is one of the ways Mennonites have helped each other in their congregations—and through CHIP, those smaller groups who cannot financially cope with health-care costs for their members.

As a caring people in our congregations we can go much beyond this basic effort. After a recent illness different members of our congregation cut our grass, repaired our mailbox and a faulty gate, offered meals—and several sent us money gifts to help with the extra heavy expenses involved. And we felt surrounded by the love and prayers of not only our Sunday school class but the congregation as a whole. There are many ways in which the traumas of tomorrow can be shared by a loving fellowship of faith.

Yet unless we live within an income-and-need-sharing Christian community we should have some ability to meet the unexpected expenses tomorrow might bring through a personal program of savings.

But many young families find it difficult to put anything aside. High fuel and energy bills and sharply higher health costs make it a problem paying for increasing grocery prices—and families of any age like to eat!

So saving isn't easy. Yet there are possibilities, even for persons on a low income. And the simplest way to begin is with a garden. Because a garden permits you to grow a variety of foodstuffs which can be dried, canned, frozen, and stored—even living in the city.

The Institute for Local Self-Reliance has demonstrated how this can happen in the Adams-Morgan area of Washington, D.C., a run-down neighborhood of turn-of-the-century townhouses and red-brick apartment buildings. The Institute was formed in 1973 to develop ways an urban community can become economically self-sustaining (see "Plowboy Interview," Vol. 36, *Mother Earth News*).

One of their major projects involves rooftop gardens, using a lightweight mixture of vermiculite and perlite as soil, light enough so that most of the roof of an apartment building can be used for intensive planting. They collect and compost vegetable wastes from community-controlled food stores, about 500 pounds a week.

Currently the group is planning a rooftop greenhouse for a senior citizens' apartment building in downtown Washington. Also they are focusing attention on the gardening potential of backyards, vacant lots—and basements, ideal for "sprouting" such nutritious items as lentils, alfalfa, or mung beans. Raising fish in basement tanks is another research project they are developing. And some ten community gardens are in operation now in vacant lots throughout their area.

Our own garden is backyard size (30' x 50') which can readily produce enough food for several small families for a year. We have fed it enormous quantities of rotting vegetable matter and maintain a dense, weed-proof mulch of old hay and scythed grass. The quantity and quality of preservable food this relatively small patch produces is astonishing. Out of it—with some wild berries we collected—Norma has established a "savings account" in our basement of over 800 quarts of vegetables, soups and soup stock, pickles, fruit, juices, jams, and jellies. In addition she has been able to give away beans, potatoes, and butternut squash in abundance, tomatoes, zucchini squash, and cucumbers. As a further bonus, the pest-controlling flowers throughout the garden are beautiful to behold.

What other "savings" besides money can you think of, from which you or your group might benefit?

Swaps and yard sales are becoming a versatile way to convert unwanted household articles into needed cash or goods.

Cooperative ownership of tools or a pickup truck is possible if a satisfactory way is devised for maintenance. One method is to establish a shared maintenance and depreciation account with each member paying in a fixed amount each month. Also for each tool each member is assigned a damage deposit which is forsaken by the individual if any breakage or irregular damage occurs while the tool or machine is in his possession. The advantage of such an arrangement is that no one person suffers all the loss of a tool, and yet a person who may have been careless pays more than others in the group.

Besides saving on the expense of the tools each might have purchased on their own, such a group is usually able to own conjointly a much wider selection of machines. In turn, this allows for savings in do-it-yourself possibilities.

A church is ideally suited to organize such ownership and provide a valuable community service. The list of possible tools can include garden tillers, carts, mowers, a truck or van, ladders, power saws, drills, routers, spray equipment, pressure canners, and a miscellany of hand tools. Such a group may also arrange to own conjointly one or more large freezers, sharing the energy expense. It can even work with laundry equipment too, with a congregational "laundromat."

Credit unions, many of them based on one or more congregations, have demonstrated how mutual savings of money can be beneficial also, while reducing the cost of borrowing for larger purchases or emergency needs.

But perhaps you have already spent yourself into a hole? How can you dig yourself out without going in deeper? Or starving to death?

Debt reduction is never easy, as many have found out to their displeasure. It is always better to control spending *before* you get into deep trouble. Yet let's explore the possibilities for you if you should find yourself behind a stack of bills you can't possibly meet on time.

First, don't panic. Decide that belt-tightening must start *now.* No further purchases except by cash—and only those that are absolutely essential to your survival.

Second, list your essential spending for the next three months.

Be sure to include any regulars such as car payments,

insurance, mortgage, utilities, etc. Determine how much is left over each month to pay on your old debts by how little you can get by on for other needs.

Now make a list of your overdue debts, beginning with the hoariest. Total them up. If what you have previously decided you can pay on your overdue accounts each month is equal to one third of your debt, you are in reasonably good shape.

Write a check for one third the amount owing, attach a brief note of explanation, and mail to your creditor. Something like this will help: "We find ourselves in a financial bind right now but I assure you we will attempt to pay the remainder as quickly as we can."

However, if you still come up short of enough for a one-third payment on your old bills, still don't reach for the panic button. If just a little more would help, ask one of your other creditors with whom you are in good standing if you can skip one month's payment of principal. Use that to make up the difference you need. If that is still not enough, try delaying the "youngest" old debt one month.

If you conscientiously aim at reducing your debts, and if you stick with a program of regular payments you will find most of your creditors will go along with you. In fact you may actually improve your credit rating with them—once your bills are paid!

The best move any of us can make is to find financial counsel within the fellowship of faith.

It would be helpful to all if your congregation were to form a financial advisory group in order to provide a wide variety of counsel in financial matters. The Lord has so constructed His body that we should be able to depend upon the members to have such care for one another. "If one member suffers, all suffer together; if one member is honored, all rejoice together" (1 Corinthians 12:26, RSV).

Once debt is under control, a program of saving can usually be managed. As we saw in the preceding chapter, budgeting consultants suggest that every family should have a savings account large enough to cover three to six months' loss of income. For many people that ideal is really an impossible dream. Unfortunately, such a frustrating suggestion often produces the opposite effect: "I can't even come close, so I won't even try."

But it is possible to put together a variety of "savings," such as we have explored in this chapter, with some cash as part of your program.

Cash savings are best achieved through controlled spending so that some money can be systematically set aside. Even small amounts set aside on a regular basis can mount up. And there is an added benefit from establishing a regular savings plan—we learn some of the disciplines of simplifying which can set us free in other areas of our lives as well.

> What would you need to survive for three months? What steps would be necessary for you to take in order to cope with an unexpected emergency or a loss of income? Who could you count on to help?

Cooperative efforts, such as group ownership, credit unions, community gardens, and the like, have the added benefit of moving us closer to caring for one another. And that is the basic difference between being anxious about the future and seeking first the kingdom of God and His righteousness.

Securing our own future without thought for others leads to the selfishness which gains the world, but loses its soul. It is good to prepare for tomorrow—if our preparations include our brothers and sisters and neighbors as well (cf. Acts 4:32-37).

The world's system wants to own us so that our lives are totally wrapped up in living to its demanding tune. But the new life which Christ can create in us moves to a different beat. Only God owns the tomorrow we are moving into—and the future of our lives can only be secured in Him.

"Never give your hearts to this world or to any of the things in it. A man cannot love the Father and love the world at the same time. For the whole world system, based as it is on men's primitive desires, their greedy ambitions and the glamour of all that they think splendid, is not derived from the Father at all, but from the world itself. The world and all its passionate desires will one day disappear. But the man who is following God's will is part of the permanent and cannot die" (1 John 2:15-17, Phillips).

Transition
From—Saving for what future?

Some futurologists warn that as social programs become more costly for wage earners a civil war may develop between wage earners and pensioners. Is mandatory retirement making that problem worse? Or does retirement make jobs available for younger people?

Learning to limit one's spending and discovering the disciplines for saving can open the door to another option: limiting one's income. What advantages might there be to a voluntarily limited income? Disadvantages? Did Jesus limit His earning power? Why? Was His an act of independence or dependence? The Apostle Paul sewed tents for a living, but without building an estate. Was he irresponsible? When does saving for the future show trust in Christ? When might it prove a lack of faith?

To—Chapter 11, Giving

Giving is part of our lives—but how much a part? We can give out of duty or compulsion, but only the motive of love brings fulfillment to a developing life of Christian commitment.

The New Testament teaches giving as a fellowship of caring, to share the abundance of God's grace. It involves the complete person—all of the gift that we are—as the expression of God's love in His world. Yet in the face of many appeals, how can we choose which demand to respond to?

Giving remains a personal choice of when to give how much to whom for what purpose. Planned giving, by faith, involves long-term giving also. Non-money gifts of possessions, time, compassion are more appropriate to certain needs. And the "neighbor" to whom we are sent can be discerned best when we are fully aware of who we are ourselves.

In chapter 11 we position the motive for giving in the love of Christ, who gave His life for us. (See 2 Corinthians 8 and 9; John 15:1-17.)

Chapter 11—Giving

A. Giving is the lifestyle of love.
   1. Handicapped neighbor gives himself.
   2. Christians have not always shown love.
   3. Only in Christ is self-giving consistently possible.

4. Christian Gentiles in Asia help Christian Jews in Jerusalem (Romans 15:27; 2 Corinthians 8).
   a. Give first of themselves to the Lord.
   b. Involves integrity of spiritual and material, the whole person.
5. God provides us enough to give (2 Corinthians 9).

B. Money is a medium of giving.
   1. When do we give?
      a. Off-the-top "first fruits" of income.
      b. Giving should be planned.
         i. Present gifts.
         ii. Deferred gifts.
   2. How much to give?
      a. The widow gave all she had.
      b. Give material goods also.
      c. Give time and compassion.
      d. Give to equalize (2 Corinthians 8:12-14).
   3. To whom?
      a. To whom is God sending us?
      b. Many unworthy voices clamor for money.
      c. Mission agencies must demonstrate ethical responsibility.
      d. Discern what will build the kingdom of God.
   4. For what purpose?
      a. Give with humility to express love of God.
      b. Jesus gave Himself for us (John 15:12-15).

11
Giving

Why, oh why, do we have such shortage of funds to carry out the church's ministry in a time of the greatest affluence Mennonites have ever experienced? I write with some sense of urgency, with deep concern and conviction, because I think this may well be my last letter to the *Gospel Herald.* As you know, I am suffering from cancer and I have a feeling within me that my time is short. This causes me to write with a great sense of urgency and deep concern because of my love for the brotherhood, my deep involvement in the life and ministry of the Mennonite Church, and my sincere belief that God has been calling us to a much-needed and a unique ministry in our time. . . .

Many of my days are spent alone here at home since I am disabled. I move about the house from room to room and look at the things that I have called ours. Some of these are quite personal. And then I realize that every one of these will soon be given up. They do not belong to me. They belong to God.

I challenge every member of the Mennonite Church to reexamine his/her own stewardship. I challenge every leader of the Mennonite Church to take a new and more objective look at the programs that are being carried out, for there is a great gap somewhere. Let us not blame one another but rather be asking, "Lord, what wilt thou have me to do?"

—Howard J. Zehr in a letter to *Gospel Herald*

David Reedy is a heavy equipment operator for a Virginia paving contractor. He puts in a lot of overtime since he can handle all of his company's various units and the low-boys to haul them. So he spends extra hours moving dozers and compactors and paving machines from job to job.

When he was a younger man, David tried to farm his home place as well. Nowadays he hasn't the time or energy to do much more than keep the fences in shape for some beef cattle and make a little hay. Because he is now trying to raise his three youngest children single-handedly too.

But little time as he has for himself, David Reedy cares for his neighbors too. Whenever a snowstorm piles into the valley, he's out with his tractor and snow blade. He opens up Ivy Moyers' barnyard and our lane, then on to Russ Patton's. Last year he took two dollars to pay for some gas, but nothing more. He has graded the gravel in our lane, cut wood for Ivy's stove, and who knows what else for other neighbors.

David Reedy is deaf. Yet in spite of his handicap, he has learned the great secret of life: to give freely of himself to others. Not out of duty or guilt or a need to establish his righteousness, but unselfishly out of the joy of his being.

Mr. Reedy is a Christian, and it would be nice to say that he cares for his neighbors just because he is a man of faith. Unfortunately, caring for neighbors isn't the automatic corollary of believing in God that we'd like it to be. History is filled with the many selfishnesses of professing Christians. Because of the close identification of Christianity and Western civilization, many of the problems in our countries are attributed to Christian principles, particularly the evils of greed and exploitation. Ascribing guilt by association, communist theoreticians have been able to persuade whole nations of peoples that Christianity induces individual selfishness rather than community concern.

But the failures of some Christians to give of themselves does not prove that Christianity is at fault, only that human selfishness is exceedingly difficult to overcome. In fact, it is the conquering of personal indifference to others which is the most impressive sign to Christians of the reality of Christ's Spirit in their lives (1 John 4:7-12).

Because for most of us giving of ourselves is the hardest thing we do, this failing continues to baffle the hopes of secular humanists and atheists and social pragmatists of all stripes. While it also frustrates the lives of Christian pastors and teachers and evangelists it is at least not totally unexpected. For they know that it is as difficult for Christian leaders to give up their own selfish instincts as for anyone else.

Yet here is where it all comes together as a wholesome lifestyle, a new humanity for the new heaven and earth. Only as Christ in us overcomes our indifference to others and brings His love to life in us, only then will life fill out its full meaning for us (Ephesians 3:14-19).

When the people of God in Jerusalem faced persecution and impoverishment, the Christians in Macedonia, Achaia, and Galatia began to experience the value of giving (Acts 24:17). Paul initiated the concern for their Jewish brethren (1 Corinthians 16:1-4) as a means of fellowship. "For if the Gentiles have come to share in their spiritual blessings, they ought also to be of service to them in material blessings" (Romans 15:27, RSV).

The church at Corinth was a young congregation and

although blessed with gifts such as tongues and prophecy, they were not fully exercising the gift of love (1 Corinthians 13). This better way Paul encouraged as the means of edification and care of each other (1 Corinthians 14:4, 12) and of reaching outsiders (1 Corinthians 14:24, 25).

A life of love for others, nurtured in the believing community, was to become the motive force behind their openhearted giving—of themselves and of their possessions. This was how it worked for the churches of Macedonia, as Paul wrote, "For in a severe test of affliction, their abundance of joy and their extreme poverty have overflowed in a wealth of liberality on their part. For they gave according to their means, as I can testify, and beyond their means, of their own free will, begging us earnestly for the favor of taking part in the relief of the saints—and this, not as we expected, but first they gave themselves to the Lord and to us by the will of God" (2 Corinthians 8:2-5, RSV).

Paul teaches them the integrity of love, that it involves the complete person, spiritual and material—for themselves and for others. As Jesus had shown His disciples through multiplying the loaves and fishes (Mark 6:41). "God is able to provide you with every blessing in abundance, so that you may always have enough of everything and may provide in abundance for every good work. As it is written: He scatters abroad, he gives to the poor; his righteousness endures for ever. He who supplies seed to the sower and bread for food will supply and multiply your resources and increase the harvest of your righteousness. You will be enriched in every way for great generosity, which through us will produce thanksgiving to God" (2 Corinthians 9:8-11, RSV).

Check the statement which seems closest to your own feelings: ____ I like to give because it feels good, ____ I give because it is expected of me, ____ I give because I need to, in order to be myself.

What do we give when we give of ourselves? Unfortunately, or so it seems, most social agencies and churches need our money as much as our time. That's how they are structured. So we can expect to be asked for money as one of the most appropriate ways we can help others in need: for mission, cancer research, emergency relief, Scripture distribution, educational needs, and the myriad demands of helping agencies doing some good to someone somewhere in this needy world today.

Then there are our own congregations and their needs. With all the clamor for funds on television and radio and arriving daily in the mail, it's little wonder our local churches suffer a drought of cash flow on occasion.

How then do we choose which appeal to respond to?

There is no question that the responsibility remains with the individual giver. Many congregations have attempted to funnel all the giving of members through a congregational giving plan, and there is much to recommend this as a method for collective channeling of the self-giving love of God. Peoples Church in Toronto has achieved widespread recognition for the united giving of its members. Their practice of raising funds through faith-promises has become a tradition with a momentum that other churches envy.

But for most of us, giving remains a personal choice of when to give how much to whom for what purpose.

1. *When?*

The Pharisee—for all that we put him down as a hypocrite—gave "off the top." That is, according to the law of Moses, he gave faithfully of the firstfruits of his income. Many of us find it easier to profit from the first-fruits of our labors, pay off our debts, and then think about giving. But the problem here is that giving isn't a primary influence in our lifestyle—looking after ourselves comes first. So we plan our buying, build up debts, and budget the debt repayment *before* we plan our giving. We put the cart before the horse, and the result is a self-serving lifestyle.

Giving *should* be planned—thought out prayerfully so that it is consistent with our life with God. We should budget our giving "off the top" of our income. And even by faith *before* we get it (1 Corinthians 16:2).

So this can involve long-term income planning too. All church agencies have deferred giving arrangements whereby we can donate a sum of money for their use now—while we receive a reasonable rate of interest to live on for the rest of our lives.

And all Christians should seriously consider giving a substantial sum—if not all—of their accumulated goods and savings (estate) to the body of Christ on their death. Again all agencies are familiar with the procedures required and can help with the details.

2. *How much?*

Everybody knows that we should give a tithe, right? And the rest is ours, right?

In the temple one day, Jesus sat down opposite the money box and watched as people put in their offerings. Many wealthy people put in large sums of money. Then a poor widow came along and dropped in two small coins. Jesus pointed this out to His disciples, and said, "I tell you, this poor widow has given more than all the others. For they gave out of their surplus. She has given all that she had to live on" (Mark 12:41-44, paraphrased).

There isn't one "right" amount to give, 10 percent or 30 percent or ____ percent. The widow gave all she had to live on, or as the Revised Standard Bible puts it, "her whole living." The Christian gives all that he is, his whole living. As the servant of God, he owns nothing— God owns all. That translates into a style of living which puts everything—wages, home, furniture, automobile— absolutely everything at the use of Christ and His body, the church.

Most of us have extra equipment we've picked up along the way—chairs we aren't using, a good shirt that's too small, extra vegetables we can grow in our gardens. All these can be useful to others—through Goodwill Industries, Mennonite Relief Sales, and similar agencies in the community.

Your compassion can be a donation too—in many instances a far more important contribution than money, as anyone who has cleaned up after an earthquake or flood in Mennonite Disaster Service can testify. In every community compassionate volunteers are welcomed at hospitals, nursing homes, agencies serving the handicapped or mentally disabled, prisons—any situation involving people in need.

Shall we give everything that we possess? Is that the rule of love? Not according to Paul's letter to the Christians at Corinth. "Provided there is an eager desire to give, God accepts what a man has; he does not ask for what he has not. There is no question of relieving others at the cost of hardship to yourselves; it is a question of equality. At the moment your surplus meets their need, but one day your need may be met from their surplus" (2 Corinthians 8:12-14, NEB).

3. *To whom?*

We are caretakers of all that is given us as servants in God's world, with the responsibility to help a particular "neighbor" who has a need that we are gifted to meet. That's why it is so important to get ourselves straightened out as to who we are and what our gifts-abilities are—because then we can see most clearly to whom it is that God has sent us, and how we are to give of ourselves in His service to them.

Unfortunately, many of us don't think of giving that way. Amos is an eastern Pennsylvania businessman who has turned a good profit every year since 1969—no small feat in the mid-seventies when the recession slowed many small businesses to a stop. Amos gives a regular portion of his tithe to his congregation. But the major share of his giving goes to a nondenominational evangelistic program which claims to save many souls by sending Bibles into communist areas in the world. This tickles Amos' fancy—a bold effort to evangelize an atheistic culture with the basic, simple message of the Bible.

"Our own mission programs don't have the same record of soul-winning. And that's where I want to put the Lord's money," Amos says firmly. But from Mennonite Broadcasts' experience in broadcasting to Russia, another picture emerges. The organization Amos gives so much money to has laid claim to converts which cannot be documented. In fact it is doubtful if they are getting Bibles into communist countries as they claim; or are engaged in any direct evangelism at all, any more than

Mennonite Broadcasts' radio programs can be called direct evangelism.

It is known that Mennonite Broadcasts' radio programs are heard. It is known that for some Christians in Russia, radio broadcasts provide the major source of scriptural teaching they receive. It is known that Vasil Magal's messages on the air are eagerly awaited and that his ministry is worth the long hours and the many dollars invested.

But the staff at Mennonite Broadcasts has accepted an ethical responsibility to claim no converts that cannot be documented. And anyone who knows the Russian situation knows that almost every new believer is won by much more than radio evangelism and Scripture distribution. While these efforts help, they are no more than tools to aid the faithful witness of the local believing community.

> How should a mission agency be evaluated? What criteria would give prospective donors an honest picture of their activity? How important are the personalities involved? Should we check each organization with our community of believers? List the reasons for and against such a plan.

I have served a number of church and social agencies as a consultant in direct mail appeals. I have seen our church agencies struggle to raise funds without bold, flashy, exciting appeals. Unfortunately, there are many others who do not operate under the same ethical restraints.

Of course people are moved by dramatic, emotional appeals. We all are. It is a hard heart indeed that will not reach for the checkbook to feed a starving child. But not all who collect the money are feeding the hungry—either with food or the bread of life.

So once again, the responsibility comes home to the individual. You must be sure that you do not misdirect what God has given into your hand to use. Don't simply respond to an emotional appeal. Consider who you are. Consider the gifts God gives to you. Consider the counsel of others, especially those who can evaluate the agency making the appeal. *Check with your congregation.* Through mutual admonition and counsel we can help each other to discern the appropriate channel for all our gifts to the building of the kingdom of God.

4. *For what purpose?*

You are responsible for your gifts. The purpose of all that has been given you is for you in turn to be the gift of God's love to your world. Not brazenly with arrogance and power, but in generous humility.

When Jesus washed the feet of His disciples, He did so to clearly demonstrate the way of generous humility in giving our gifts to others. It is so easy for us to give with strings attached in order to pressure people in the direction we want them to go.

But humility does not expect a return. Love gives love without a demand. Gifts are freely given to express only one purpose: the loving generosity of God. "God shows his love for us in that while we were yet sinners Christ died for us" (Romans 5:8).

Humility is not steeped in feelings of guilt either. We do not give love out of a sense of guilt, because love is not a duty nor a penance to be paid. In Christ we are set free of guilt and penance in order to love freely.

Love provides its own drive to serve, its own eager motivation to lay down its life for its friends. The world sees such love not as humility but humiliation. Yet love knows better.

Total giving of oneself is never easy. But it is the unique way of Christ. "This is my commandment, that you love one another as I have loved you," Jesus told His disciples. "Greater love has no man than this, that a man lay down his life for his friends. You are my friends if you do what I command you. No longer do I call you servants, for the servant does not know what his master is doing; but I have called you friends, for all that I have heard from my Father I have made known to you" (John 15:12-15, RSV).

The humility of loving service raises the servant into friendship with Jesus, who gave Himself for us all.

What greater purpose can we have for our lives? What richer friendship can be found?

Transition

From—Giving

Analyze your giving: do you know at this moment how much of your paycheck is available for others? Have you consulted anyone on who is the "neighbor" who needs your gift? Who would you talk to about giving: _____ pastor, _____ teacher, _____ Christian friends, _____ church treasurer?

When you give, does it feel as if it is something you do because you should? Does it feel as if it is important to you? Necessary as part of your lifestyle? A response to God? In one sense, giving because it is expected can teach us the deeper meaning of giving because we are alive in the love of God.

How much more of you is yet to be set free as a gift in and for God's world? Are you afraid to give, afraid to be used up? Can love cast out that fear also? (see 1 John 4:18). When? How?

To—Chapter 12, The church organizes its resources

The presence of Christ can be visible in our communities through His body, the church. Yet local congregations often substitute ritual for effective ministry. "Worship services" can move us further from living out the presence of Christ—if our weekday lifestyles are not worshipful service.

The Apostle Paul describes a life of reasonable worship to the Roman Christians which is both personal and a part of the community of believers—as the incarnation of God's love to our neighbors. An evaluation of our congregational program therefore is the first step in increasing our effectiveness together.

Individual members want to be involved in the decisions of where their resources are used. So, as congregations, we need to make room for each other's opinions and hear one another's concerns for mission and service. A revised Sunday morning schedule is suggested to provide time for congregational planning and processing of resources.

Then five fundamentals of how people give are explored to help congregations organize their resources.

In Chapter 12 the objective is to move toward individual involvement in congregational mission: Using resources in reasonable service to the community which is our spiritual worship. (See Romans 12; John 17:20-23; Ephesians 5:18-21.)

Chapter 12—The church organizes its resources

A. Church is a unique organization.
   1. Capable of greater works than Jesus (John 14:12).
      a. His presence among us (Matthew 18:15-20).
      b. Perfect unity in Trinity (John 17:20-23).
      c. In spite of our failings, the church will triumph.
   2. Combines our integrated lifestyles.
      a. "Worship" is our dedication of total lifestyle.
      b. Combines witness of Christ's character in His body.

B. Church organizes resources.
1. Evaluation of programs.
2. Restructure Sunday service.
   a. Preaching the work of the Lord.
   b. Planning together the work.
   c. Personal study of the work.
3. Fundamentals of giving.
   a. Law of intense competition.
   b. Law of donor participation.
   c. Law of adequate information.
   d. Law of rational-emotional appeal.
   e. Law of now.

12
The church organizes its resources

Why should young people be so dead set against "organization" in the church when some of man's most fantastic feats—the Apollo moon flights, relief flights to Biafra, and massive immunization campaigns against polio—have been accomplished by "organization"? Why is organization "good" in such efforts but "bad" in the church? Part of this reaction may be due to the impersonal character that much organization takes on, with decisions made at the top, far removed from grass-roots feelings. But the main cause of this disillusionment is probably that too often church organization itself has become the goal, rather than a means to reach the goal . . . so much church time seems to be spent spinning wheels that are going nowhere. Sensitive laymen, who in business are accustomed to hard decisions about what is really working and what is not, throw up their hands in dismay when they see programs which have long ago outlived their usefulness continued in the church for sentiment's or old time's sake.

If the church has been called to glorify God by winning men to Christ, building them up in the faith, and sending them out to witness and serve, then surely periodic studies should be made to see if the organization is serving these ends or serving itself.

—Leighton Ford in *One Way to Change the World*

The church of Jesus Christ is the most remarkable entity the world has ever known, *because it is the living presence of God in the world.* That is why Jesus told His disciples they would be capable of greater works than He (John 14:12) because where two or three are gathered to bind or loose a problem, He is there (Matthew 18:15-20). And it is the power of God in full measure, not only as made visible in Jesus, but in all possible configurations of the incarnation of God: Father, Son, and Spirit. As Jesus prayed, "I do not pray for these only, but also for those who believe in me through their word, that they may all be one; even as thou, Father, art in me, and I in thee, that they also may be in us, so that the world may believe that thou hast sent me. The glory which thou hast given me I have given to them, that they may be one even as we are one, I in them and thou in me, that they may be-come perfectly one, so that the world may know that thou hast sent me and hast loved them even as thou hast loved me" (John 17:20-23, RSV).

The church—your congregation and mine—has the potential of becoming the incarnation of God in our com-munities, if—if Christ is allowed to break through the hardness of our wills to be the head of His body.

Not all congregations are freed up from the world. In Revelation 2 and 3 Christ speaks the word of judgment to seven churches—some actively struggling to free themselves of the world, some weakening in the struggle. And one which thinks it has arrived but has actually failed, saying, "I have prospered, and I need nothing," not knowing that it is "wretched, pitiable, poor, blind, and naked" (Revelation 3:17, RSV).

How can we tell where our congregation is in its strug-gle with the world? By examining ourselves first. By be-coming ourselves a loving servant of the church first so that we can understand what the Spirit of God is doing in and among His people.

It is easy to criticize a congregation, far easier than it is to understand what God wants to work out in its members. A church is a peculiar entity, living stones built into a house in which God lives (1 Peter 2) in order to be light in a darkened world (1 John 1:5, 6; Matthew 5:14-16). But because the world in which we are familiar residents is so glitteringly dark it is hard for us to decide precisely where its glitter ends and where the true light begins.

Perhaps that is the reason why we like to keep our churches the way they are. Or if we make any changes, we copy the "successful" churches with a bus ministry or a beautiful new sanctuary or an evangelistic program that works.

But these are rituals. We look down on Tibetan prayer wheels as instruments of ritual, empty of spiritual vitality. Yet an emphasis on programs can be just as ritualistic—and empty. We can gather together, meeting after meeting, in rich rituals of singing and preaching and worship, yet be moving away from rather than closer to living obedience to Christ our Lord.

In writing the Christians at Rome, the veteran church builder Paul sums up his experience and his teaching. And in Romans 12, he pulls together his understanding of worship by the people of God. In this chapter he touches again on the picture he has of the church as one body, as he describes it also to the Christians at Corinth and in Asia (1 Corinthians 12:12 f.; Ephesians 2:16; Colossians 3:15). And he explains that the worship of the people of God is not a ritual gathering on the first day of the week but a total, integrated lifestyle, holy (dedicated) and acceptable to God. Paul then describes how this act of integrated dedication (Romans 12:1) becomes service to God—both rationally and spiritually our true worship—through the daily acts of our lives.

It is individual yet corporate, personal worship, yet functioning within the worshiping community. Paul talks of our bodies within the one body of Christ, operating as a united whole through our individual gifts: not only speaking for God (v. 6) but also serving His world (v. 7), teaching of His reality and activity, and urging people to accept the gospel (v. 8).

But there is more. Not only is our integrated lifestyle one of proclaiming His gospel and showing His life in a "religious" sense, but also in our working lives and community relationships. We are to express individually—as the worship of the church collectively—the love of God *through how we live among our neighbors*. Sharing our money and possessions freely and liberally. Giving aid to others cheerfully (v. 8).

Furthermore, if our neighbors give us a hard time for our faith, this living service to God will show the church to be forgiving, merciful, peace-loving, harmonious, sympathetic, humble, and appreciative of whatever is good; overcoming evil in a positive way (vv. 9-12).

This is how the church worships, by serving God faithfully. Only then can we avoid being ritually self-serving as we sing and fellowship together. Such meetings are not "service," as we often call them, nor should we label them "worship"—because they are only a small part of our rational service and spiritual worship as the people of God.

> Take a survey: which do most people think of as "worship service"—a meeting in a church? Or as Paul teaches in Romans 12, the life of the church as it serves in the world? Why?

Many of our congregations still measure spiritual vitality by the number of meetings their members attend. Yet there is little reason for anyone to harass a congregation for lack of attendance at meetings when a relatively simple evaluation might show that other activities or helps would be well received.

Evaluation of our program and resources is the first step in becoming more effective as the people of God.

"I bid every one among you," Paul urged the congregation at Rome, "not to think of himself more highly than he ought to think, but to think with sober judgment" (Romans 12:3, RSV). Evaluation is one of the better tools we have to help us. If we'll use it.

How do the members perceive the congregation in relation to their daily lives? Is there a process or means for each member to explain his or her work, aims, and problems? Or is the congregation still majoring in "listener-speaker" style programs?

Does the congregation provide resources and guidance for the vocational and avocational decisions of its members? Do members feel they are being equipped for *their* ministry in the body of Christ (Ephesians 4:12)? Here should be the goal of your congregational programs as a fundamental means to attaining "the unity of the faith and of the knowledge of the Son of God, to mature manhood, to the measure of the stature of the fulness of Christ" (Ephesians 4:13, RSV).

Does each member feel involved in the congregational mission? Are their lives an intimate part of mission? Do you attempt together to reach out beyond yourselves with time and money gifts. Is each member adequately involved in the overall goals of the agency to which you are giving?

Many church leaders despair at the amount of money going outside the denomination to agencies which appeal to members directly. The questions arise, "Are our members voting against our programs with their checkbooks? Or are we just not making the work of our agencies attractive enough?"

It is biblically sound and psychologically consistent to expect people to want to be involved where their resources are put to work. In advising the agencies which I serve as direct mail fund-raising consultant, this is the point at which we begin to build a program. It seems such an obvious fact that we need not argue for its acceptance. But it is nevertheless largely ignored in most congregations in favor of unspecified or general giving toward the budget.

It is interesting that while many congregations try the "faith-promise" method of giving (used by some congregations which are renowned for their large mission programs), most fail in the attempt. Because the "faith-promise" way (pledging to give large sums in faith that God will provide) depends for its success on thoroughly acquainting the congregation with each mission activity, each relief project, each evangelistic program, each activity to be supported.

That takes time. And we have so many other things to do. When we do have a report from a mission or service agency it is often handled as something "extra" to be squeezed in Sunday morning and thus blamed for making people late for dinner.

So when an interesting, personally involving mission does get the attention of our members (a large number do) it is no surprise to me that the eager-to-serve heart responds in loving generosity.

Estimate what proportion of your congregational giving goes into _____ congregational needs, _____ local mission, _____ local service, _____ world mission, _____ world service. Which would you change? How?

Since most congregations find it difficult to arrange schedules to meet as a total group at any time other than Sunday morning, it is time for a change in the use of that most hallowed period. Instead of two one-hour chunks, break it in three 40-minute periods, moving from the general to the specific.

1. *Preaching the Work of the Lord:* after the invocation (a psalm, hymn, and/or prayer) go directly into the sermon. Move into the next period with singing.

2. *Planning the Work of the Lord:* here the congregation becomes more involved together in processing the working Word: in planning program, verifying expenditures, setting up operational groups, confirming gifts, discerning direction, hearing mission and service representatives, deciding response, etc. This segment needs to be well-orchestrated by a responsible leader with a team to help in its various areas. And while children could move into their classes before this period begins, the rest of the congregation—youth and hoary head—are needed in the processes involved.

Conclude by receiving tithes and offerings.

3. *Personalizing the Work of the Lord:* after a song, break into study classes to further process the working Word. Here biblical study and practical fellowship can interpret the Spirit's direction for individuals in their lives.

There are several good reasons to provide the time for

congregational processing which is not normally made available by the kind of schedules we now live by. In addition to opening up time for planning congregational needs as a total group (something that rarely happens in most churches) it provides for personal stewardship of resources within the community of believers. We can see each other in action as we reveal our values—between families, across generations, within differing economic positions. And that experience can be as important to us as the singing we share together.

> How much would you be interested in others' patterns of giving? _____ not interested, _____ moderately interested in knowing why others give as they do, _____ very interested in helping me shape my own stewardship ideals.

There are at least five fundamentals or "laws" about how people give for a congregation to recognize in organizing their resources:

1. *The law of intense competition.* There are many needs coming at us from all sides today. Members should be encouraged to speak for those which appeal to them. And our own Mennonite agencies should be clearly explained and advocated. If we can't change our Sunday morning services for regular input, we should at least plan a Mission Exploration Sunday each quarter. This would set aside both teaching and preaching hours for well-planned advocacy and open discussion of a broad range of service and mission opportunities.

2. *The law of donor participation.* This needs emphasizing again and again. While some person may give to a congregational budget because it is mandated, unity

of purpose will be considerably enhanced if each member participates frequently in the selection and reaffirmation of mission projects to be supported.

A wise congregation will allow room for individually favored projects also. With the wide range of Spirit-inspired talents we can expect in any congregation, we must expect similarly wide-ranging interests in mission. No one should be made to feel his giving to a project is "outside" of his congregation's life—not if he is truly encouraged to represent his congregation in such gifts.

3. *The law of adequate information.* This fundamental is never forgotten in mail appeals for funds. No one gives to a need that isn't adequately and interestingly explained. Yet if anything is said before lifting the offering in church it is most often a complaint that "we aren't meeting our budget." Nothing could be more disheartening.

This comes from the mistaken idea that our "worship service" is sufficiently motivating to stimulate mission involvement throughout the week and mission giving on Sunday. That most of us in the pews experience frustration in the one and lack of motivation in the other should be obvious. But the obvious isn't always easy to see.

Every Mennonite agency tries to feed information to the people through the *Gospel Herald* and other printed materials. Yet the most effective process—and the most beneficial for the people of God—is to see this as a vital aspect of our "reasonable service" or "spiritual worship" (Romans 12:1). So congregational planning to provide adequate information—and discussion about it—is absolutely necessary. And the impulse to dedicated involvement in the rest of our lives should happen to us through some kind of regular participation Sunday mornings.

4. *The law of rational-emotional approval.* Mennonites like to think they give of themselves rationally rather than emotionally. This seems to be particularly true of the younger generation of well-trained professionals who may see something weak in emotional responses.

Yet when push comes to shove it is only irrationally emotional appeals which Mennonites reject. Love is not empty of emotion (God deliver us from any "love" that does not include our emotions!) nor of rational commitment. I suggest that when reason is satisfied we respond best to those appeals which also gain our emotional approval.

So when a pastor reproves a congregation for not meeting its budget he is doing the worst possible thing he could do. Rather than scold at the end of the quarter, begin the quarter with a rationally sensible and emotionally involving presentation of "what we are doing together in God's world—and what more can be done if we continue to work together with all our different gift-abilities and the inspiring love of God."

It can also be argued that we aren't always as rational as we think we are. Many a congregation has talked itself into a building program as the "rational" thing to do when the old building is too small—without a thorough exploration of alternative solutions to their needs. It is a sorry indictment of our rational creativity if we simply follow what others have done in investing in more brick and mortar. Particularly when mission and service agencies are running short of funds.

5. *The law of now.* Now is the acceptable time of jubilee. Now is the hour of salvation. Now is the time to set
aside my gifts for today's needs—and now is the time to
anticipate tomorrow's situations.

Giving to an annual fund or a budget projection is
about as dry as a popcorn sandwich—and as satisfying.
Christ's mission isn't projections, it's people. Living, suffering, dying-too-soon people who are lonely now, are
hungry and in prison now. Planning together for our personal involvement can take on its fullest meaning only if
it is specifically in the present tense.

Every long-range project has a present direction—
something we tend to lose sight of. Only by examining
the now of a project can we be guided freely by the Spirit
of God into newer directions. And that happens as we explore its potential together.

> How do you judge an appeal? ____ by the value of the
> service it offers, ____ by an opinion of the spiritual integrity
> of the people involved, ____ by judging the kingdom work
> performed, ____ by how I respond to the claims made, ____
> by how others recommend the work?

The process of giving of ourselves is delightfully
many-sided. As we make room for each other, reinforce
each other in obeying Christ, encourage each other in
living service—which is our spiritual worship—we grow
together in the fullness of God. And in the full joy of
maturing Christlikeness.

This is the mutuality of being together in the body of
Christ—seeing in each other the working out of God's
purpose. And helping that purpose to happen.

". . . let the Spirit stimulate your souls. Express your
joy in singing among yourselves psalms and hymns and

spiritual songs, making music in your hearts for the ears of God! Thank God at all times for everything, in the name of our Lord Jesus Christ. And 'fit in with' one another, because of your common reverence for Christ" (Ephesians 5:18-21, Phillips).

Transition
From—The church organizes its resources

Many of us see ourselves as separate from others and only members of a group incidentally and voluntarily. But this does not apply to the church of Jesus Christ. If by faith we belong to Christ we also belong to His body, the church, whether we are fully aware of it or not. How does this change the way you perceive your role in life? If you are given abilities and gifts and interests, then these are a part of the resources of the body of Christ, not only where you live, but also in the world at large. Including your dollars and your possessions.

What is your procedure for putting all that you are at the disposal of Christ? Are you the sole judge of what you should or should not do? Or has your local congregation a voice in the matter? What about other Christians in your community? Christ speaks through His Spirit, but also through His people—of all denominations. So when do you say "no," to whom, and why? How do you say "yes"?

To—Chapter 13, Celebrating life

What God has begun He will bring to fruition, and it is the Christian's glory to share in His purposes for His creation. For the difficulties of everyday living we have been given the faith to survive, more, to triumph in joy. And a simplifying lifestyle is our celebration.

Our faith is sufficient for our responsibilities. We all have faith enough—and more than enough—to do what we know must be done. So in a litany of 10 reasons, we complete a renewed commitment to the simplified lifestyle of Christ.

In Chapter 13 our purpose is to apply our reason and our faith in a celebration of renewal. See Luke 17:1-10.

Chapter 13—Celebrating life

A. Celebration from beginning to end.
   1. In the beginning life, in the end renewed life (John 1).
   2. In the beginning the glory of the Word; in the end, glory shared (John 14).

B. Celebrating in the harshness of today.
   1. By faith doing what our talents are called to do in duty (Luke 17:1-10).
   2. Translates in justice for the poor and for the earth.

C. Celebrating lifestyles are shared.
   1. With each other in congregation.
   2. With our Lord.

D. Ten reasons for a focused lifestyle.

13
Celebrating life

To you we owe our hymn of praise, O God in Zion;
To you must vows be fulfilled, you who hear prayers.
To you all flesh must come because of wicked deeds.
We are overcome by our sins; it is you who pardon them.
Happy the man you choose, and bring to dwell in your
    courts.
May we be filled with the good things of your house, the
    holy things of your temple!

With awe-inspiring deeds of justice you answer us, O God
    our savior,
The hope of all the ends of the earth and of the distant seas.
You set the mountains in place by your power, you who are
    girt with might;
You still the roaring of the seas, the roaring of their waves
    and the tumult of the peoples.
And the dwellers at the earth's ends are in fear at your
    marvels;
the farthest east and west you make resound with joy.

You have visited the land and watered it; greatly have you
    enriched it.
God's watercourses are filled; you have prepared the grain.
Thus have you prepared the land; drenching its furrows,
    breaking up its clods,
Softening it with showers, blessing its yield.
You have crowned the year with your bounty, and your
    paths overflow with a rich harvest;

> The untilled meadows overflow with it, and rejoicing
> clothes the hills.
> The fields are garmented with flocks and the valleys
> blanketed with grain. They shout and sing for joy.
>   —Psalm 65, *The New American Bible*

In the beginning God created the heavens and the earth. In the end a new heaven and a new earth. In the beginning, God. In the end, God surrounded by His people.

"And behold, a great multitude which no man could number, from every nation, from all tribes and peoples and tongues, standing before the throne and before the Lamb, clothed in white robes, with palm branches in their hands, and crying out with a loud voice, 'Salvation belongs to our God who sits upon the throne, and to the Lamb!' " (Revelation 7:9, 10, RSV).

In the beginning, the great celebration of life. In the end the celebration of renewed life, made greater by the reconciling work of Christ, the Lamb of God, "who takes away the sin of the world!" (John 1:29).

In the beginning was the glory of the Word. "And the Word became flesh and dwelt among us, full of grace and truth; we have beheld his glory, glory as of the only Son from the Father" (John 1:14, RSV).

In the end is the glory shared. "Let not your hearts be troubled," Jesus said, "believe in God, believe also in me. . . . Truly, truly, I say to you, he who believes in me will also do the works that I do; and greater works than these will he do, because I go to the Father. Whatever you ask in my name, I will do it, that the Father may be glorified in the Son . . . By this my Father is glorified, that you bear much fruit, and so prove to be my disciples. As the Father has loved me, so have I loved you; abide in my love . . . that my joy may be in you, and that your joy may be full'' (John 14:1, 12, 13; 15:8, 9, 11, RSV).

The people of God share the glory of God in being fruitful, serving Him and His creation. And the incredible joy which fills us to overflowing is ours as we love one another.

The church of Jesus Christ gives its life for the world in each generation. This is the love with which Christ loved us and gave Himself for us. And this is the love with which we love one another. A lifestyle of love in giving ourselves to Christ and to His body in the world.

> Consider in the light of your own emotional highs and lows what it could mean to you to share the glory of Jesus. Which one or more might best describe it for you? _____ exciting, _____ satisfying, _____ enriching, _____ humbling, _____ challenging, _____ frustrating, _____ consciousness raising, _____ conscience awakening, _____ ego stimulating, _____ ego shattering, _____ fulfilling.

How do such heavenly understandings get translated into earthly realities? How do you love somebody you can barely get along with? How can we find joy in a congregation that is only infrequently enjoyable? What is to celebrate in a life beset with complicated frustrations?

Christians aren't spared the traumas of living. In fact it is the difficulties in surviving—physically and psychically—which provide us the experiences through which our faith is exercised. Because unless our faith grows accustomed to trusting God, we will continue to trust our family ties or wealth or professional skills.

Many religiously minded people think of faith as an add-on, an accessory by which we can miraculously remove the hardships in living and the problems of loving. That may be what the apostles sought when they said to the Lord, "Increase our faith!" (See Luke 17:1-10.)

Jesus' answer seems steeped in irony. Faith isn't a matter of size, He tells them, and needn't be any larger than a tiny mustard seed. At least, not to do miracles like telling a tree to uproot itself and be planted in the sea. Because moving mountains isn't what life is about, as Jesus points out. The real problems are instead how to forgive a person who persists in wronging you, time after time, even seven times in a day (Luke 17:4).

In the harsh experiences of loving people who may not want to be loved, we need the faith that His way is the right way. And Jesus tells the disciples that they already know more about that kind of faith than they are living. He goes on to describe the situation of the servant who works in the field, then comes in and makes his master's dinner before sitting down to his own meal. The servant has only done what he knows is expected of him.

"So you also," Jesus reminds us, "when you have done all that is commanded you, say, 'We are unworthy servants; we have only done what was our duty' " (Luke 17:10, RSV).

> If it is true, as Jesus says, that we have faith to do more than we are already doing, what might that mean for your life? What is there now in your life that should change—attitudes, habits, feelings toward others—in order to become more like Christ? What is preventing you from making those changes by faith now?

Today our faith has much duty to do in order to bear fruit. The gospel of jubilee for the poor seeks to find an adequate translation through our lifestyles. Justice is the practical expression of the love we are called to share. Even the earth cries out for the righteous acts of those who know to do more than they are doing.

And so our celebration takes on the determined joy of the forgiven penitent: "Thy will be done in earth, as it is in heaven." Thy will be done in me, Lord. I give over all that I am and have in order that whatever You have gifted me to do will be done.

The joys of our celebrating lifestyles are shared rejoicings. What we do with our gifts and resources is done in the body of faith also. "Thy will be done" is a shared prayer, to *our* Father, who forgives *us* our debts, as *we* forgive our debtors. Together our gifts are multiplied in feeding the bread of life to a hungering multitude.

We may not be sure what it is our dutiful faith can accomplish. But we must try by putting our gifts to work in faith—and with the skillful encouragement of the church. We need to experiment in faith. Practice loving and giving in more effective ways, combining our gifts in the body of Christ for an enriched ministry in the world.

How will we know if what we do is an appropriate ministry? The only evidence we may see may be a look of renewed hope in eyes tired with defeat. A promise of renewed beauty shining out of bleak misery—faith doesn't need much more than that to go on. As David, the hero in Elizabeth Goudge's novel *Bird in the Tree*, says, "Faith is the belief in something that you don't understand yet, and beauty is the evidence that the thing is there."

So the lifestyle we are putting on by faith is the Word from which love and justice and forgiveness can speak life. As the Spirit of God breathes through His body, His life-giving gifts and fruits appear. Through these He recreates in us the person of Jesus. From Him the church's mission draws its strength and direction. The Holy Spirit has made holiness the goal of creation—and our mission together is to be His breath moving upon the waters of re-creation.

Together we celebrate our meaning, our shared purpose. We help each other—almost in spite of ourselves. But as love grows its strength in us, we grow to care less for our differences and more for the diversity among us. Each Christian among us brings a wealth of cultural insight for our mutual surrender to Christ. And as we each free the other to become, we all are freed to mature in that lifestyle which is Christ.

> If wholesome holiness is the goal God has in mind for the church, what freedom do you still need in order to contribute wholesomeness to the community of faith? As you consider the areas in your life which may yet need to be conformed to Christ, remember to celebrate the areas He has already set free. He has begun a work in you which He will not abandon. You can count on His help—and the help of His body—to work with you in becoming the responsible Christian that He wants you to be.

In a guest editiorial in *Gospel Herald*, Edgar Metzler shared some insights from Jorgen Lissner of the Lutheran World Federation. He listed ten reasons for Christians to move toward a simpler focused lifestyle. As Lissner says, we may simplify our lives out of guilt, or as a substitute for political action, or in the quest of moral purity. Whatever the reason, he sees two important side effects: economic adjustments throughout the world with benefits for rich and poor alike. And the release of new resources and energies for social change.

Adapting his reasons to our own litany of celebration,

let us complete our renewed commitment to the lifestyle
of Christ:

> Our Lord and our God, we take up Your simplifying
> lifestyle
>
> *as an act of belief* in the power of Your love to free us from
> ourselves and our sins and to set us on the course of a new
> life that cares for others;
>
> *as an act of faith* in the integrity of Your concern for the
> poor and our commitment to a more equitable distribu-
> tion of the world's resources;
>
> *as an act of self-defense* against the mind-polluting effects
> of overconsumption;
>
> *as an act of withdrawal* from the achievement-neurosis of
> our high-pressure materialistic societies;
>
> *as an exercise of purchasing power* to redirect production
> away from the satisfaction of artifically created wants
> toward the supply of goods and services that meet
> genuine social needs;
>
> *as an act of provocation* to arouse curiosity leading to dia-
> logue with others about affluence, alienation, poverty,
> and social injustice;
>
> *as an act of advocacy* of social, political, and economic
> changes which can lead to jubilee;
>
> *as an act of solidarity* with the majority of humankind,
> which has no choice about lifestyle;
>
> *as an act of sharing* with others what has been given to us, or
> of returning what was usurped by us through unjust
> social and economic structures;
>
> *as an act of celebration* of the riches found in creativity,
> spirituality, and community with others.

For our sufficiency, holy Father, we thank You—
strengthen our resolve to share our resources with others,
whoever they might be.

For our life, holy Son, we thank You—encourage our
determination to live responsibly in Your world,
whatever might be the need.

For our love, holy Spirit, we thank You—broaden our hearts to love all who would be our neighbors, wherever they might live.

And we shall give You praise, now with our lives, and forever with our loving service. Amen.

Appendix:
Psychosocial tests

Numerous psychosocial tests are available to help identify abilities, talents, gifts, and interests. This list is only a sampling—but these are perhaps among the best.

Hall Occupational Orientation Inventory. L. G. Hall and R. B. Tarrier, Scholastic Testing Service, Inc., 480 Meyer Road, Bensenville, IL 60106. An excellent tool that approaches occupational interests and abilities from the individual's inner self, rather than the external "job hunter." It is self-scored and thus helps with self-evaluation. It views work as a way of achieving meaning and fulfillment in life.

The Hall instrument comes in the Young Adult/College edition which is used with all adult age groups. An Adult Basic edition is intended for those whose literacy level is lower than average.

Planning for Work, Self-Guidance Series, by Miriam H. Krohn, director of Counselor Relations, Catalyst, 6 East 82nd St., New York, NY 10028—1973. Best series of self-evaluation helps for women, particularly those returning to the job market or combining career and family responsibilities.

Strong-Campbell Interest Inventory and the new *Career-Assessment Inventory* are both available from National Computer Systems, Inc., 4401 West 76th Street, Minneapolis, MN 55435.

Both of these are more job-market oriented than the Hall, assessing interests which can point to specific occupations. The individual's interests are assessed and compared (by a computer) with the interests of satisfied workers in various occupations, which gives a good indication of the individual's potential for achievement and satisfaction in those occupations. Score sheets must be processed through National Computer Systems Inc.

Time and Talent Program, Dwight E. Newberg, Nashville: Cokesbury Press, 1976. An innovative plan developed by the United Methodist Church to focus on the release and development of every member's talent. Purpose: to get people involved in the work of the church.

Vocational Exploration Groups, a system for career selection in groups produced by Studies for Urban Man Inc., P. O. Box 1039, Tempe, AZ 85281.

For further reading

Allen, Donald R., *Barefoot in the Church*. Richmond, Va.: John Knox Press, 1972. The story of Trinity Presbyterian, an unusual congregation and their caring ministries, with reference to a variety of like "communities" around the world.

Becker, Palmer, *Congregational Goals Discovery Plan* (with leader's guide). Newton, Kan.: General Conference Mennonite Church, 1976. An illustrated guide to a comprehensive survey and program for developing congregational goals for the purpose of carrying them out in specific actions.

Bell, Carolyn Shaw, *The Economics of the Ghetto*. New York: Pegasus, 1970.

Bolles, Richard Nelson, *What Color Is Your Parachute?* Box 4310, Berkeley, Calif. 94704: Ten Speed Press, 1975. A practical manual for life planning. Excellent resource for an unusual congregation and their caring ministries, and of a variety of like "communities" around the world.

Bonhoeffer, Dietrich, *The Cost of Discipleship*. London: S.C.M. Press, Ltd., 1959. Classic text on living in Christ in a disciplined, focused life.

Callahan, Daniel J., ed., *The Secular City Debate*. New York: Macmillan, 1966. A collection of critical essays from *Commonweal, Christianity and Crisis*, and *Christian Century* on Cox's book, plus Cox's responses. Helpful balance and expansion of the problems we face in tomorrow's if not today's world.

Clark, M. Edward, ed., *The Church Creative*. Nashville: Abingdon Press, 1967. A reader on the renewal of the church as seen in 18 various social experiences across the United States.

Cobb, John B., *Is It Too Late?* Beverly Hills, Calif.: Bruce, 1972. A theology of ecology.

Cox, Harvey, *The Secular City*. New York: Macmillan, 1965. Secularization and urbanization in a positive theological perspective. Note section on the emancipation of work from "religion": how society wrongly defines work only in terms of market skills.

Crystal, John C. and Bolles, Richard N., *Where Do I Go from Here with My Life?* New York: Seabury Press, 1974. The companion study guide (for individuals as well as groups) to *What Color Is Your Parachute?* Excellent resource; designed for individual use, use with counselor, use in small groups.

Dulles, Avery, S. J., *Models of the Church*. Garden City, N.Y.: Doubleday and Co., Inc., 1972. A basic definition of "church" and a critical assessment of its directions in five "models."

Employment and Voluntary Opportunities for Older People. Free from National Clearinghouse on Aging, Washington, D.C. 20201.

Gish, Arthur G., *Beyond the Rat Race*. Scottdale, Pa.: Herald Press, 1973. Argument for a focused lifestyle from Church of the Brethren author.

Guinness, "Os," *The Dust of Death*. Downers Grove, Ill.: Inter-Varsity Press, 1973. A Christian response to *Future Shock*.

Hecht, Miriam and Traub, Lillian, *Alternative to College*. New York: Macmillan, 1974. Helpful for those who can benefit from careers not needing a degree.

Jeschke, Marlin, *Discipling the Brother*. Scottdale, Pa.: Herald Press, 1972. Explores the difficult areas of mutual admonition—an Anabaptist heritage that has almost been abandoned.

Kauffman, Milo, *Stewards of God*. Scottdale, Pa.: Herald Press, 1975. Study of stewardship by one of leading Mennonite thinkers on the subject. Particularly thorough explanation of the tithe.

Larson, Bruce, *The Relational Revolution*. Waco, Tex.: Word Books, 1976. Larson recently concluded a research project on relational theology, funded by Lilly Endowment. Emphasizes the major resource of persons in the church.

Mother Earth News. P. O. Box 70, Hendersonville, N.C. 28739, 6-issues-a-year magazine which has exemplified the return to a simple lifestyle.

Nicholls, William, ed., *Conflicting Images of Man.* New York: Seabury Press, 1966. Brief survey of philosophical and religious views of humanity.

O'Connor, Elizabeth, *Eighth Day of Creation.* Waco, Tex.: Word Books, 1971. The vitality of the church in focusing the lives of its members on serving Christ.

Peters, Victor, *All Things Common: The Hutterian Way of Life.* New York: Harper and Row, 1965. Worthwhile for the thorough exploration of an Anabaptist communal way of discipleship.

Pincus, John A., ed., *Reshaping the World Economy.* Englewood Cliffs, N.J.: Prentice-Hall, 1968. Essays by a number of economists, with some conference reports which set the problems of rich and poor nations in perspective and attempt some directions for the future.

Redekop, Calvin, *The Free Church and Seductive Culture.* Scottdale, Pa.: Herald Press, 1970. A pertinent view of the pressures of our world and the response of the church.

Richards, Lawrence O., *Three Churches in Renewal.* Grand Rapids, Mich.: Zondervan, 1975. A case history of three very different churches committed to expressing the body of Christ through the exercise of the gifts of individual members in community with other believers.

Rosen, Sumner M., ed., *Economic Power Failure: The Current American Crisis.* New York: McGraw-Hill, 1975. Essays and reports covering a broad perspective of current economic problems: oil, multinationals, shifts in world economies, unemployment, taxation, the military—with some observations for the future. Includes Barry Commoner, Arthur Burns, E. F. Schumacher, Ralph Nader.

Schaller, Lyle E., *The Churches War on Poverty.* Nashville: Abingdon Press, 1967. How the Christian church can cooperate with government to work in practical local situations by mobilizing resources, written in the social optimism of the mid-sixties.

Schumacher, E. F., *Small Is Beautiful*. New York: Harper and Row, 1973. Economics from the point of view of simplified, community-oriented systems rather than large-scale production which can profit only a few.

Shortney, Joan Ranson, *How to Live on Nothing*. New York: Pocket Books, 1968 (revised 1971, original by Doubleday, 1961). The title is fulfilled many times over in this ultimate how-to-do-it book for the simpler lifestyle.

Singh, Surjit, *Communism, Christianity, Democracy*. Richmond, Va.: John Knox Press, 1965. The comparisons of secularized versions of Christianity in Marxism-Leninism and liberal democracy with a Christianity that still saves.

Sinha, Radha, *Food and Poverty: The political economy of confrontation*. New York: Holmes and Meier Publishers, 1976. A critical analysis of current approaches to development, population control, and agricultural methods for the poorer countries by a senior lecturer in economics at the University of Glasgow.

Stringfellow, William, *Free in Obedience*. New York: Seabury Press, 1964. A vigorous argument by a lay-theologian for the radical Christian life.

Taylor, David E., ed., *99 Ways to a Simple Lifestyle*. 1757 S. Street Northwest, Washington, D.C. 20009 Center for Service in the Public Interest, 1976. A full-of-ideas report with items on heating and cooling, other home conserving methods, food, gardening, solid waste, clothing, fulfillment, health, transportation, community interest.

Theobold, Robert, *Free Men and Free Markets*. Garden City, N.Y.: Doubleday, 1965. An argument for redistribution of wealth through a guaranteed annual income.

Toffler, Alvin, *Future Shock*. New York: Random House, 1970. Most widely read of the "future books." Focuses our attention on directions which our responses to technology are taking us. Illustrates the frustrations of limited adaptation to changes forced upon us, and how we might learn to cope with the future.

Ward, Barbara, *The Lopsided World*. New York: W. W. Norton, 1968. The renowned socioeconomist looks at the disparities between rich and poor countries.

What Shall I Order for Our Career Planning and Placement Library? P. O. Box 2263, Bethlehem, Pa. 18001: College Placement Council Inc. An annual bibliography of publications ranked in three sections for small, medium, and large libraries. Keeps up-to-date on materials in the field.

Ziegler, Edward K., *Simple Living*. Elgin, Ill.: Brethren Press, 1974. The past experiences and present condition of the Church of the Brethren in regard to disciplined living.

Early in his business career, **James Fairfield** developed a profit-sharing program for the employees of the plant in which he worked, "perhaps the most significant thing I ever did in the textile industry," he reports.

Today as a fund-raising consultant to a growing number of church and social agencies, he has developed some positive methods for helping people take charge of their own lives. And that includes their spending habits, savings plans, and patterns of giving.

Jim and Norma Fairfield operate Creative Counselors from their home in Virginia's Shenandoah Valley, visited often by their four married children.

He is also the author of *When You Don't Agree* (Herald Press, 1977).